the w. chan kim &
renée mauborgne
blue ocean
strategy
reader

THE ICONIC ARTICLES BY
THE BESTSELLING AUTHORS OF
BLUE OCEAN STRATEGY

the w. chan kim &
renée mauborgne
blue ocean
strategy
reader

Harvard Business Review Press

Boston, Massachusetts

Copyright 2017 Harvard Business School Publishing Corporation
All rights reserved
Printed in the United States of America
10 9 8 7 6 5 4 3 2 1

The web addresses referenced in this book were live and correct at the time of the book's publication but may be subject to change.

Library of Congress Cataloging-in-Publication Data

Names: Kim, W. Chan, author. | Mauborgne, Renée, author.
Title: The W. Chan Kim and Renée Mauborgne Blue Ocean Strategy reader / by W. Chan Kim and Renée Mauborgne.
Description: Boston, Massachusetts : Harvard Business Review Press, [2017]
Identifiers: LCCN 2016040913 | ISBN 9781633692749 (pbk.)
Subjects: LCSH: New products. | Market segmentation.
Classification: LCC HF5415.153 .K533 2017 | DDC 658.8/02—dc23
    LC record available at https://lccn.loc.gov/2016040913

ISBN: 978-1-63369-274-9
eISBN: 978-1-63369-275-6

The paper used in this publication meets the requirements of the American National Standard for Permanence of Paper for Publications and Documents in Libraries and Archives Z39.48-1992.

Contents

the w. chan kim &
renée mauborgne
blue ocean
strategy
reader

Introduction

BLUE OCEAN STRATEGY is one of the most influential business ideas of our time. The award-winning eponymous book by W. Chan Kim and Renée Mauborgne, first published in 2005 and reissued in an expanded edition in 2015, has become a global phenomenon—selling over 3.6 million copies worldwide and available in forty-four languages. The idea is popular in companies across the globe because it addresses the one challenge that, irrespective of geography or industry, all managers eventually face: how to create new market space.

But what most managers may not know is that Kim and Mauborgne's theory, frameworks, and tools for creating new market space were first published in the pages of *Harvard Business Review* as groundbreaking articles that redefined how managers should think about and execute strategy. Defying the conventional wisdom, these articles challenged the notion of competition as the focus of strategy. Instead, they argued, head-to-head competition leads to imitation strategies and shrinks the profit pool. To grow profitably, companies should break free from competition with rivals by staking out fundamentally new market space. These articles also rejected the widely accepted idea that strategy is essentially a choice between differentiation and low cost. One of the central tenets of the blue ocean concept is the simultaneous pursuit of both differentiation and low cost—that a company's actions can favorably affect both cost structure *and* its value proposition to buyers instead of trading off between them. Taken all together, these articles formed the basis for what eventually became known as *blue ocean strategy*.

This volume finally brings those pieces together—along with the *Harvard Business Review* articles Kim and Mauborgne published after the book's debut, which extend the ideas of blue ocean strategy further. With this book, readers now have the quintessential blue ocean strategy concepts and tools in their most fundamental form. Presented in the order in which they were originally published, the articles in this volume provide an unprecedented view into how the ideas and tools evolved and offer managers a new way to work with the ideas—starting with the first critical step of changing how your company thinks about strategy to ultimately ensuring that your blue ocean strategy is a success. Whether or not you're already familiar with *Blue Ocean Strategy*, this collection of articles will give you another perspective on these widely accepted theory, frameworks, and tools—and help you implement them in your organization.

Piece by piece, these articles delve into the unconventional strategic mindset that defines a blue ocean strategy and explain the systematic process for changing your company's strategic focus, identifying new opportunities, creating a new value curve, building a profitable business model, and overcoming organizational hurdles. The articles also introduce the analytic tools—the Value Curve and the Strategy Canvas, the Six Paths Framework, the Four Actions Framework, the Pioneer-Migrator-Settler Map, the Buyer Utility Map, the Price Corridor of the Mass, and the Business Model Guide—that companies the world over use to formulate and execute a blue ocean strategy. Understanding the concepts, processes, and tools in these articles is critical for strategy teams, organizational leaders, and anyone who is charged with implementing strategy.

Challenge your strategic logic: The first article in the collection introduces the concept that became the cornerstone of blue ocean strategy. In **"Value Innovation: The Strategic Logic of High Growth,"** Kim and Mauborgne find that what separates high-growth companies from the rest of the pack is how they think about strategy—what questions managers ask, what opportunities they see and pursue, and how they understand risk. Managers in most companies focus on matching or beating rivals (the conventional logic of strategy), whereas managers in high-growth companies seek to create products or services for which there are no direct competitors. Because the latter group succeeds by creating *leaps in value* for customers instead of by benchmarking against the competition, the authors coined the term *value innovation* to describe this fundamentally different strategic logic. With examples such as Accor and Virgin Atlantic, this article introduces two tools for changing the strategic logic of your team: the Value Curve, which charts a company's relative performance across its industry's key success factors, and the

Pioneer-Migrator-Settler Map, which assesses a company's portfolio of businesses for growth opportunities.

Use a fair process: Distrust and lack of engagement often result when managers launch major change efforts without inviting employees' input. But evidence shows that most people will accept outcomes not wholly in their favor, *if* they believe the process for arriving at those outcomes was fair. **"Fair Process: Managing in the Knowledge Economy"** shows how a poor process can ruin the outcome of even a good decision and offers three principles—engagement, explanation, and expectation clarity—that together lead to judgments of fair process and help companies channel people's energy and creativity toward organizational goals.

Find uncontested markets: Creating new market space requires a different pattern of strategic thinking, but managers often don't know where to start. In **"Creating New Market Space,"** Kim and Mauborgne offer a practical way to pursue value innovation by systematically looking across the conventionally defined boundaries of competition: across substitute industries, strategic groups, buyer groups, complementary product and service offerings, the functional-emotional orientation of an industry—and even across time. Introducing the tool now known as the Six Paths Framework (referring to these six ways for thinking beyond accepted boundaries), this article shows how to create new market space by reconstructing market boundaries, using examples such as Home Depot, Intuit, Polo Ralph Lauren, Bloomberg, and Starbucks. The article also applies the Value Curve tool to chart the way a company or an industry configures its offerings to customers, and introduces the Eliminate, Reduce, Raise, Create tool (what has come to be known as the Four Actions Framework) for creating a new value curve.

Identify which idea has real commercial potential: Once a company has identified potential new market spaces, the challenge for executives is knowing which ones to pursue. Three tools—the Buyer Utility Map, the Price Corridor of the Mass, and the Business Model Guide—together offer a systematic way to reduce uncertainty. **"Knowing a Winning Business Idea When You See One"** explains how each tool works and illustrates them through several company examples such as Schwab, Southwest Airlines, and Swatch.

Visualize your new strategy: Introducing the iconic Strategy Canvas tool, an analytic framework that is central to value innovation and the creation of blue oceans, **"Charting Your Company's Future"** shows how to draw a visual picture of your strategy that's easy to understand and communicate and engages people across the organization. The authors demonstrate how to draw a strategy canvas, using a structured process they call the Four Steps of Visualizing Strategy—visual awakening, visual exploration, visual strategy fair, and visual communication—and use in-depth examples of the short-haul airline industry and a European financial services company to illustrate the process.

Overcome the organizational hurdles: With any shift in strategy, especially toward blue oceans that represent a departure from the status quo, leaders face a number of hurdles: cognitive, resource-related, motivational, and political (a framework the authors call the Four Hurdles to Execution). **"Tipping Point Leadership"** shows how to overcome them all and bring about rapid, dramatic change—at low cost and while winning employees' backing.

Put it all together: In **"Blue Ocean Strategy,"** the first article to unveil the idea and coin the term, Kim and Mauborgne reveal their Red Ocean vs. Blue Ocean Strategy framework. Bringing together the research findings, underlying concepts, and unique logic that forms the basis of their theory, Kim and Mauborgne explain what is and what isn't a blue ocean strategy and show how to apply blue ocean strategic moves.

Shape your business environment: Building on the underlying differences between red oceans and blue oceans, this article explains that there are fundamentally two types of strategy: *structuralist* strategies that assume the operating environment is a given (a common red ocean assumption) and *reconstructionist* strategies that seek to shape the environment (such as a blue ocean strategy). While the structuralist approach is valuable and relevant (red oceans will always exist), the reconstructionist approach is more appropriate in certain economic and industry settings. **"How Strategy Shapes**

Structure" explains how to choose the right approach and, for whichever strategy you choose, how to align three strategy propositions: a value proposition that attracts buyers, a profit proposition that enables the company to make money out of the value proposition, and a people proposition that motivates those working for or with the company to execute the strategy.

Unleash your organization's talent: A main cause of employee disengagement is poor leadership. Yet no manager sets out to be a poor leader. The problem is that many managers lack a clear understanding of what it would take to bring out the best in everyone and achieve high impact. Leaders can gain this understanding through an approach Kim and Mauborgne call *blue ocean leadership.* The article **"Blue Ocean Leadership"** uses the core concepts and tools of blue ocean strategy—such as the Leadership Canvas (an adaptation of the Strategy Canvas) and the Eliminate, Reduce, Raise, Create Grid—to look at what leaders actually do and at which acts and activities they could do differently to boost both people's motivation and business results. Designed to be used at all levels—top, middle, and frontline—the tools in this article extend the leadership capabilities and unleash previously unexploited talent and energy in organizations.

Ensure that your market-creating strategy is a success: After analyzing blue ocean successes and failures for more than a decade, Kim and Mauborgne identified a common factor that seems to consistently undermine the execution of market-creating strategies—the mental models of the managers involved in them. In their research, the authors encountered six especially salient assumptions built into managers' mental models that effectively keep them anchored in red oceans and prevent them from entering blue oceans of uncontested market space. **"Red Ocean Traps"** looks at each trap in detail and helps managers avoid getting caught in them.

Blue ocean strategy is among the rarest of business ideas in that its significant global impact reaches not only to the everyday world of managers grappling with how to transform their companies, but also to the academic world, where it is taught at over eighteen hundred universities worldwide. Because it is grounded in data, systematic in its approach, and supported by a number of analytical tools and frameworks, it's easy to see why academics as well as managers are drawn to it. Yet as powerful as these systematic ideas and tools are, formulating a blue ocean strategy is ultimately a creative act. It's about seeing your world differently and unleashing the creativity of the people in your organization. What could be more invigorating and rewarding?

—The Editors

Value Innovation

The Strategic Logic of High Growth

AFTER A DECADE OF DOWNSIZING and increasingly intense competition, profitable growth is a tremendous challenge many companies face. Why do some companies achieve sustained high growth in both revenues and profits? In a five-year study of high-growth companies and their less successful competitors, we found that the answer lay in the way each group approached strategy. The difference in approach was not a matter of managers choosing one analytical tool or planning model over another. The difference was in the companies' fundamental, implicit assumptions about strategy. The less successful companies took a conventional approach: Their strategic thinking was dominated by the idea of staying ahead of the competition. In stark contrast, the high-growth companies paid little attention to matching or beating their rivals. Instead, they sought to make their competitors irrelevant through a strategic logic we call value innovation.

Consider Bert Claeys, a Belgian company that operates movie theaters. From the 1960s to the 1980s, the movie theater industry in Belgium was declining steadily. With the spread of videocassette recorders and satellite and cable television, the average Belgian's movie going dropped from eight to two times per year. By the 1980s, many cinema operators (COs) were forced to shut down.

The COs that remained in business found themselves competing head-to-head for a shrinking market. All took similar actions. They turned cinemas into multiplexes with as many as ten screens, broadened their film offerings to attract all customer segments, expanded their food and drink services, and increased showing times.

Those attempts to leverage existing assets became irrelevant in 1988, when Bert Claeys created Kinepolis. Neither an ordinary cinema nor a multiplex, Kinepolis is the world's first megaplex, with 25 screens and 7,600 seats. By offering moviegoers a radically superior experience, Kinepolis won 50% of the market in Brussels in its first year and expanded the market by about 40%. Today, many Belgians refer not to a night at the movies but to an evening at Kinepolis.

Consider the differences between Kinepolis and other Belgian movie theaters. The typical Belgian multiplex has small viewing rooms that often have no more than 100 seats, screens that measure seven meters by five meters, and 35-millimeter projection equipment. Viewing rooms at Kinepolis have up to 700 seats, and there is so much legroom that viewers do not have to move when someone passes by. Bert Claeys installed oversized seats with individual armrests and designed a steep slope in the floor to ensure everyone an unobstructed view. At Kinepolis, screens measure up to 29 meters by ten meters and rest on their own foundations so that sound vibrations are not transmitted among screens. Many viewing rooms have 70-millimeter projection equipment and state-of-the-art sound equipment. And Bert Claeys challenged the industry's conventional wisdom about the importance of prime, city-center real estate by locating Kinepolis off the ring road circling Brussels, 15 minutes from downtown. Patrons park for free in large, well-lit lots. (The company was prepared to lose out on foot traffic in order to solve a major problem for the majority of moviegoers in Brussels: the scarcity and high cost of parking.)

Bert Claeys can offer this radically superior cinema experience without increasing ticket prices because the concept of the megaplex results in one of the lowest cost structures in the industry. The average cost to build a seat at Kinepolis is about 70,000 Belgian francs, less than half the industry's average in Brussels. Why? The megaplex's location outside the city is cheaper; its size gives it economies in purchasing, more leverage with film distributors, and better overall margins; and with 25 screens served by a central ticketing and lobby area, Kinepolis achieves economies in personnel and overhead.

Idea in Brief

Struggling to stay ahead of your rivals? No need. Instead of trying to match or beat them on cost or quality, make the other players irrelevant—by staking out new market space where competitors haven't ventured.

How? Become a **value innovator:** identify radical ideas that make quantum leaps in the value you provide customers.

Value innovators ask, "What if we started fresh—and forgot everything we know about our industry's existing rules and traditions?" When CNN's creators asked this question, they replaced the traditional networks' format with real-time news from around the world, 24 hours a day.

Value innovators don't set out to build competitive advantage. But their innovative practices lead them to achieve precisely that. Virgin Atlantic, for example, cut first-class airline service and channeled cost savings into greater value for business-class passengers: more comfortable seats and free transportation to and from airports. It attracted not only business-class customers but also full-economy-fare and first-class passengers of other airlines.

Furthermore, the company spends very little on advertising because its value innovation generates a lot of word-of-mouth praise.

Within its supposedly unattractive industry, Kinepolis has achieved spectacular growth and profits. Belgian moviegoers now attend the cinema more frequently because of Kinepolis, and people who never went to the movies have been drawn into the market. Instead of battling competitors over targeted segments of the market, Bert Claeys made the competition irrelevant. (See the exhibit "How Kinepolis achieves profitable growth.")

Why did other Belgian COs fail to seize that opportunity? Like the others, Bert Claeys was an incumbent with sunk investments: a network of cinemas across Belgium. In fact, Kinepolis would have represented a smaller investment for some COs than it did for Bert Claeys. Most COs were thinking—implicitly or explicitly—along these lines: The industry is shrinking, so we should not make major investments—especially in fixed assets. But we can improve our performance by outdoing our rivals on each of the key dimensions of competition. We must have better films, better services, and better marketing.

Idea in Practice

To become a value innovator, consider the following strategies, as exemplified by French hotelier Accor:

Assume that you can shape your industry's conditions. In the mid-1980s, the budget hotel industry in France had two markets: inexpensive hotels that had poor beds and noise, and pricier hotels that provided upscale amenities and a decent night's sleep. Accor redefined the industry by providing inexpensive *and* superior accommodations to cost-conscious travelers.

Focus on what the majority of your buyers value. Accor identified what customers of all budget hotels wanted: a good night's sleep for a low price.

Consider how you might change your offering to capture the market you've identified. Eliminate features that offer no value for customers—or that detract from

---

How Kinepolis achieves profitable growth

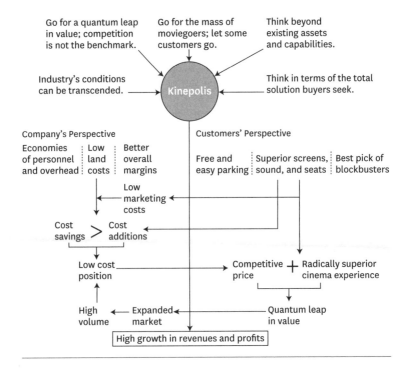

4

value. Simplify products or services that have been overdesigned in the race to match or beat rivals. Further improve high-value features so that customers no longer have to make compromises. And create new features that your industry has never offered.

> **Example:** Accor created an entirely new hotel concept: its Formule 1 line of budget hotels. The company eliminated costly restaurants and lounges, reckoning that target customers could do without them. It reduced other features; for example, providing receptionists only during peak check-in and check-out hours, and replacing closets and dressers with a few shelves and a pole for clothing. And it improved several features—for instance, providing good sound insulation by building rooms with low-cost modular blocks.

Bert Claeys followed a different strategic logic. The company set out to make its cinema experience not better than that at competitors' theaters but completely different—and irresistible. The company thought as if it were a new entrant into the market. It sought to reach the mass of moviegoers by focusing on widely shared needs. In order to give most moviegoers a package they would value highly, the company put aside conventional thinking about what a theater is supposed to look like. And it did that while reducing its costs. That's the logic behind value innovation.

Conventional Logic versus Value Innovation

Conventional strategic logic and the logic of value innovation differ along the five basic dimensions of strategy. Those differences determine which questions managers ask, what opportunities they see and pursue, and how they understand risk. (See the exhibit "Two strategic logics.")

Industry assumptions

Many companies take their industries' conditions as given and set strategy accordingly. Value innovators don't. No matter how the rest of the industry is faring, value innovators look for blockbuster ideas

Two strategic logics

The five dimensions of strategy	Conventional logic	Value innovation logic
Industry assumptions	Industry's conditions are given.	Industry's conditions can be shaped.
Strategic focus	A company should build competitive advantages. The aim is to beat the competition.	Competition is not the benchmark. A company should pursue a quantum leap in value to dominate the market.
Customers	A company should retain and expand its customer base through further segmentation and customization. It should focus on the differences in what customers value.	A value innovator targets the mass of buyers and willingly lets some existing customers go. It focuses on the key commonalities in what customers value.
Assets and capabilities	A company should leverage its existing assets and capabilities.	A company must not be constrained by what it already has. It must ask, What would we do if we were starting anew?
Product and service offerings	An industry's traditional boundaries determine the products and services a company offers. The goal is to maximize the value of those offerings.	A value innovator thinks in terms of the total solution customers seek, even if that takes the company beyond its industry's traditional offerings.

and quantum leaps in value. Had Bert Claeys, for example, taken its industry's conditions as given, it would never have created a megaplex. The company would have followed the endgame strategy of milking its business or the zero-sum strategy of competing for share in a shrinking market. Instead, through Kinepolis, the company transcended the industry's conditions.

Researching the Roots of High Growth

DURING THE PAST FIVE YEARS, we have studied more than 30 companies around the world in approximately 30 industries. We looked at companies with high growth in both revenues and profits and companies with less successful performance records. In an effort to explain the difference in performance between the two groups of companies, we interviewed hundreds of managers, analysts, and researchers. We built strategic, organizational, and performance profiles. We looked for industry or organizational patterns. And we compared the two groups of companies along dimensions that are often thought to be related to a company's potential for growth. Did private companies grow more quickly than public ones? What was the impact on companies of the overall growth of their industry? Did entrepreneurial start-ups have an edge over established incumbents? Were companies led by creative, young radicals likely to grow faster than those run by older managers?

We found that none of those factors mattered in a systematic way. High growth was achieved by both small and large organizations, by companies in high-tech and low-tech industries, by new entrants and incumbents, by private and public companies, and by companies from various countries.

What did matter—consistently—was the way managers in the two groups of companies thought about strategy. In interviewing the managers, we asked them to describe their strategic moves and the thinking behind them. Thus we came to understand their views on each of the five textbook dimensions of strategy: industry assumptions, strategic focus, customers, assets and capabilities, and product and service offerings. We were struck by what emerged from our content analysis of those interviews. The managers of the high-growth companies—irrespective of their industry—all described what we have come to call the logic of value innovation. The managers of the less successful companies all thought along conventional strategic lines.

Intrigued by that finding, we went on to test whether the managers of the high-growth companies applied their strategic thinking to business initiatives in the marketplace. We found that they did.

Furthermore, in studying the business launches of about 100 companies, we were able to quantify the impact of value innovation on a company's growth in both revenues and profits. Although 86% of the launches were line extensions—that is, incremental improvements—they accounted for 62% of total revenues and only 39% of total profits. The remaining 14% of the launches—the true value innovations—generated 38% of total revenues and a whopping 61% of total profits.

Strategic focus

Many organizations let competitors set the parameters of their strategic thinking. They compare their strengths and weaknesses with those of their rivals and focus on building advantages. Consider this example. For years, the major U.S. television networks used the same format for news programming. All aired shows in the same time slot and competed on their analysis of events, the professionalism with which they delivered the news, and the popularity of their anchors. In 1980, CNN came on the scene with a focus on creating a quantum leap in value, not on competing with the networks. CNN replaced the networks' format with real-time news from around the world, 24 hours a day. CNN not only emerged as the leader in global news broadcasting—and created new demand around the globe—but also was able to produce 24 hours of real-time news for one-fifth the cost of one hour of network news.

Conventional logic leads companies to compete at the margin for incremental share. The logic of value innovation starts with an ambition to dominate the market by offering a tremendous leap in value. Value innovators never say, Here's what competitors are doing; let's do this in response. They monitor competitors but do not use them as benchmarks. Hasso Plattner, vice chairman of SAP, the global leader in business application software, puts it this way: "I'm not interested in whether we are better than the competition. The real test is, will most buyers still seek out our products even if we don't market them?"

Because value innovators don't focus on competing, they can distinguish the factors that deliver superior value from all the factors the industry competes on. They do not expend their resources to offer certain product and service features just because that is what their rivals are doing. CNN, for example, decided not to compete with the networks in the race to get big-name anchors. Companies that follow the logic of value innovation free up their resources to identify and deliver completely new sources of value. Ironically, even though value innovators do not set out to build advantages over the competition, they often end up achieving the greatest competitive advantages.

Customers

Many companies seek growth through retaining and expanding their customer bases. This often leads to finer segmentation and greater customization of offerings to meet specialized needs. Value innovation follows a different logic. Instead of focusing on the differences between customers, value innovators build on the powerful commonalities in the features that customers value. In the words of a senior executive at the French hotelier Accor, "We focus on what unites customers. Customers' differences often prevent you from seeing what's most important." Value innovators believe that most people will put their differences aside if they are offered a considerable increase in value. Those companies shoot for the core of the market, even if it means losing some of their customers.

Assets and capabilities

Many companies view business opportunities through the lens of their existing assets and capabilities. They ask, Given what we have, what is the best we can do? In contrast, value innovators ask, What if we start anew? That is the question the British company Virgin Group put to itself in the late 1980s. The company had a sizable chain of small music stores across the United Kingdom when it came up with the idea of music and entertainment megastores, which would offer customers a tremendous leap in value. Seeing that its small stores could not be leveraged to seize that opportunity, the company decided to sell off the entire chain. As one of Virgin's executives puts it, "We don't let what we can do today condition our view of what it takes to win tomorrow. We take a clean slate approach."

This is not to say that value innovators never leverage their existing assets and capabilities; they often do. But, more important, they assess business opportunities without being biased or constrained by where they are at a given moment. For that reason, value innovators not only have more insight into where value for buyers resides—and how it is changing—but also are much more likely to act on that insight.

Product and service offerings

Conventional competition takes place within clearly established boundaries defined by the products and services the industry traditionally offers. Value innovators often cross those boundaries. They think in terms of the total solution buyers seek, and they try to overcome the chief compromises their industry forces customers to make—as Bert Claeys did by providing free parking. A senior executive at Compaq Computer describes the approach: "We continually ask where our products and services fit in the total chain of buyers' solutions. We seek to solve buyers' major problems across the entire chain, even if that takes us into a new business. We are not limited by the industry's definition of what we should and should not do."

Creating a New Value Curve

How does the logic of value innovation translate into a company's offerings in the marketplace? Consider the case of Accor. In the mid-1980s, the budget hotel industry in France was suffering from stagnation and overcapacity. Accor's cochairmen, Paul Dubrule and Gérard Pélisson, challenged the company's managers to create a major leap in value for customers. The managers were urged to forget everything they knew about the existing rules, practices, and traditions of the industry. They were asked what they would do if Accor were starting fresh.

In 1985, when Accor launched Formule 1, a line of budget hotels, there were two distinct market segments in the industry. One segment consisted of no-star and one-star hotels, whose average price per room was between 60 and 90 French francs. Customers came to those hotels just for the low price. The other segment was two-star hotels, with an average price of 200 Fr per room. Those more expensive hotels attracted customers by offering a better sleeping environment than the no-star and one-star hotels. People had come to expect that they would get what they paid for: Either they would pay more and get a decent night's sleep, or they would pay less and put up with poor beds and noise.

Accor's managers began by identifying what customers of all budget hotels—no star, one star, and two star—wanted: a good night's sleep for a low price. Focusing on those widely shared needs,

Accor's managers saw an opportunity to overcome the chief compromise that the industry forced customers to make. They asked themselves the following four questions: Which of the factors that our industry takes for granted should be eliminated? Which factors should be reduced well below the industry's standard? Which factors should be raised well above the industry's standard? Which factors should be created that the industry has never offered?

The first question forces managers to consider whether the factors that companies compete on actually deliver value to consumers. Often those factors are taken for granted, even though they have no value or even detract from value. Sometimes what buyers value changes fundamentally, but companies that are focused on benchmarking one another do not act on—or even perceive—the change. The second question forces managers to determine whether products and services have been overdesigned in the race to match and beat the competition. The third question pushes managers to uncover and eliminate the compromises their industry forces customers to make. The fourth question helps managers break out of the industry's established boundaries to discover entirely new sources of value for consumers.

In answering the questions, Accor came up with a new concept for a hotel, which led to the launch of Formule 1. First, the company eliminated such standard hotel features as costly restaurants and appealing lounges. Accor reckoned that even though it might lose some customers, most people would do without those features.

Accor's managers believed that budget hotels were overserving customers along other dimensions as well. On those, Formule 1 offers less than many no-star hotels do. For example, receptionists are on hand only during peak check-in and checkout hours. At all other times, customers use an automated teller. Rooms at a Formule 1 hotel are small and equipped only with a bed and the bare necessities—no stationery, desks, or decorations. Instead of closets and dressers, there are a few shelves and a pole for clothing in one corner of the room. The rooms themselves are modular blocks manufactured in a factory, a method that results in economies of scale in production, high quality control, and good sound insulation.

Formule 1 gives Accor considerable cost advantages. The company cut in half the average cost of building a room, and its staff costs dropped from between 25% and 35% of sales—the industry average—to between 20% and 23%. Those cost savings have allowed Accor to improve the features customers value most to levels beyond those of the average French two-star hotel, but the price is only marginally above that of one-star hotels.

Customers have rewarded Accor for its value innovation. The company has not only captured the mass of French budget hotel customers but also expanded the market. From truck drivers who previously slept in their vehicles to businesspeople needing a few hours of rest, new customers have been drawn to the budget category. Formule 1 made the competition irrelevant. At last count, Formule 1's market share in France was greater than the sum of the five next largest players.

The extent of Accor's departure from the standard thinking of its industry can be seen in what we call a value curve—a graphic depiction of a company's relative performance across its industry's key success factors. (See the exhibit "Formule 1's value curve.") According to the conventional logic of competition, an industry's value curve follows one basic shape. Rivals try to improve value by offering a little more for a little less, but most don't challenge the shape of the curve.

Like Accor, all the high-performing companies we studied created fundamentally new and superior value curves. They achieved that through a combination of eliminating features, creating features, and reducing and raising features to levels unprecedented in their industries. Take, for example, SAP, which was started in the early 1970s by five former IBM employees in Walldorf, Germany, and became the worldwide industry leader. Until the 1980s, business application software makers focused on subsegmenting the market and customizing their offerings to meet buyers' functional needs, such as production management, logistics, human resources, and payroll.

While most software companies were focusing on improving the performance of particular application products, SAP took aim at the

Formule 1's value curve

Formule 1 offers unprecedented value to the mass of budget hotel customers in France by giving them much more of what they need most and much less of what they are willing to do without.

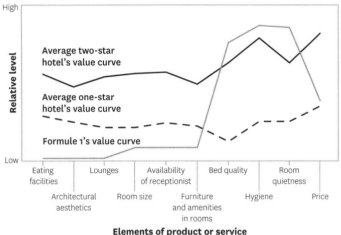

Elements of product or service

mass of buyers. Instead of competing on customers' differences, SAP sought out commonalities in what customers value. The company correctly hypothesized that for most customers, the performance advantages of highly customized, individual software modules had been overestimated. Such modules forfeited the efficiency and information advantages of an integrated system, which allows real-time data exchange across a company.

In 1979, SAP launched R/2, a line of real-time, integrated business application software for mainframe computers. R/2 has no restriction on the platform of the host hardware; buyers can capitalize on the best hardware available and reduce their maintenance costs dramatically. Most important, R/2 leads to huge gains in accuracy and efficiency because a company needs to enter its data only once. And R/2 improves the flow of information. A sales manager, for example, can find out when a product will be delivered and why it is late by cross-referencing the production database. SAP's growth and profits have exceeded its industry's. In 1992, SAP achieved a new value innovation with R/3, a line of software for the client-server market.

The Trap of Competing, the Necessity of Repeating

What happens once a company has created a new value curve? Sooner or later, the competition tries to imitate it. In many industries, value innovators do not face a credible challenge for many years, but in others, rivals appear more quickly. Eventually, however, a value innovator will find its growth and profits under attack. Too often, in an attempt to defend its hard-earned customer base, the company launches offenses. But the imitators often persist, and the value innovator—despite its best intentions—may end up in a race to beat the competition. Obsessed with hanging on to market share, the company may fall into the trap of conventional strategic logic. If the company doesn't find its way out of the trap, the basic shape of its value curve will begin to look just like those of its rivals.

Consider this example. When Compaq Computer launched its first personal computer in 1983, most PC buyers were sophisticated corporate users and technology enthusiasts. IBM had defined the industry's value curve. Compaq's first offering—the first IBM-compatible PC—represented a completely new value curve. Compaq's product not only was technologically superb but also was priced roughly 15% below IBM's. Within three years of its launch, Compaq joined the *Fortune* 500. No other company had ever achieved that status as quickly.

How did IBM respond? It tried to match and beat Compaq's value curve. And Compaq, determined to defend itself, became focused on beating IBM. But while IBM and Compaq were battling over feature enhancements, most buyers were becoming more sensitive to price. User-friendliness was becoming more important to customers than the latest technology. Compaq's focus on competing with IBM led the company to produce a line of PCs that were overengineered and overpriced for most buyers. When IBM walked off the cliff in the late 1980s, Compaq was following close behind.

Could Compaq have foreseen the need to create another value innovation rather than go head-to-head against IBM? If Compaq had monitored the industry's value curves, it would have realized that by the mid- to late 1980s, IBM's and other PC makers' value curves were converging with its own. And by the late 1980s, the curves were nearly identical. That should have been the signal to Compaq that it was time for another quantum leap.

Monitoring value curves may also keep a company from pursuing innovation when there is still a huge profit stream to be collected from its current offering. In some rapidly emerging industries, companies must innovate frequently. In many other industries, companies can harvest their successes for a long time; a radically different value curve is difficult for incumbents to imitate, and the volume advantages that come with value innovation make imitation costly. Kinepolis, Formule 1, and CNN, for example, have enjoyed uncontested dominance for a long time. CNN's value innovation was not challenged for almost ten years. Yet we have seen companies pursue novelty for novelty's sake, driven by internal pressures to leverage unique competencies or to apply the latest technology. Value innovation is about offering unprecedented value, not technology or competencies. It is not the same as being first to market.

When a company's value curve is fundamentally different from that of the rest of the industry—and the difference is valued by most customers—managers should resist innovation. Instead, companies should embark on geographic expansion and operational improvements to achieve maximum economies of scale and market coverage. That approach discourages imitation and allows companies to tap the potential of their current value innovation. Bert Claeys, for example, has been rapidly rolling out and improving its Kinepolis concept with Metropolis, a megaplex in Antwerp, and with megaplexes in many countries in Europe and Asia. And Accor has already built more than 300 Formule 1 hotels across Europe, Africa, and Australia. The company is now targeting Asia.

The Three Platforms

The companies we studied that were most successful at repeating value innovation were those that took advantage of all three platforms on which value innovation can take place: product, service, and delivery. The precise meaning of the three platforms varies across industries and companies, but in general, the product platform is the physical product; the service platform is support such as maintenance, customer service, warranties, and training for distributors and retailers; and the delivery platform includes logistics and the channel used to deliver the product to customers.

Too often, managers trying to create a value innovation focus on the product platform and ignore the other two elements. Over time, that approach is not likely to yield many opportunities for repeated value innovation. As customers and technologies change, each platform presents new possibilities. Just as good farmers rotate their crops, good value innovators rotate their value platforms. (See the sidebar "Virgin Atlantic: Flying in the Face of Conventional Logic.")

The story of Compaq's server business, which was part of the company's successful comeback, illustrates how the three platforms can be used alternately over time to create new value curves. (See the exhibit "How Has Compaq Stayed on Top of the Server Industry?") In late 1989, Compaq introduced its first server, the SystemPro, which was designed to run five network operating systems—SCO UNIX, OS/2, Vines, NetWare, and DOS—and many application programs. Like the System-Pro, most servers could handle many operating systems and application programs. Compaq observed, however, that the majority of customers used only a small fraction of a server's capacity. After identifying the needs that cut across the mass of users, Compaq decided to build a radically simplified server that would be optimized to run NetWare and file and print only. Launched in 1992, the ProSignia was a value innovation on the product platform. The new server gave buyers twice the SystemPro's file-and-print performance at one-third the price. Compaq achieved that value innovation mainly by reducing general application compatibility—a reduction that translated into much lower manufacturing costs.

Virgin Atlantic: Flying in the Face of Conventional Logic

WHEN VIRGIN ATLANTIC AIRWAYS CHALLENGED its industry's conventional logic by eliminating first-class service in 1984, the airline was simply following the logic of value innovation. Most of the industry's profitable revenue came from business class, not first class. And first class was a big cost generator. Virgin spotted an opportunity. The airline decided to channel the cost it would save by cutting first-class service into value innovation for business-class passengers.

First, Virgin introduced large, reclining sleeper seats, raising seat comfort in business class well above the industry's standard. Second, Virgin offered free transportation to and from the airport—initially in chauffeured limousines and later in specially designed motorcycles called LimoBikes—to speed business-class passengers through snarled city traffic.

With those innovations, which were on the product and service platforms, Virgin attracted not only a large share of the industry's business-class customers but also some full economy fare and first-class passengers of other airlines. Virgin's value innovation separated the company from the pack for many years, but the competition did not stand still. As the value curves of some other airlines began converging with Virgin's value curve, the company went for another leap in value, this time from the service platform.

Virgin observed that most business-class passengers want to use their time productively before and between flights and that, after long-haul flights, they want to freshen up and change their wrinkled clothes before going to meetings. The airline designed lounges where passengers can take showers, have their clothes pressed, enjoy massages, and use state-of-the-art office equipment. The service allows busy executives to make good use of their time and go directly to meetings without first stopping at their hotels—a tremendous value for customers that generates high volume for Virgin. The airline has one of the highest sales per employee in the industry, and its costs per passenger mile are among the lowest. The economics of value innovation create a positive and reinforcing cycle.

When Virgin first challenged the industry's assumptions, its ideas were met with a great deal of skepticism. After all, conventional wisdom says that in order to grow, a company must embrace more, not fewer, market segments. But Virgin deliberately walked away from the revenue generated by first-class passengers. And it further rejected conventional wisdom by conceiving of its business in terms of customer solutions, even if that took the company well beyond an airline's traditional offerings. Virgin has applied the logic of value innovation not just to the airline industry but also to insurance, music, and entertainment retailing. The company has always done more than leverage its existing assets and capabilities. It has been a consistent value innovator.

How has Compaq stayed on top of the server industry?

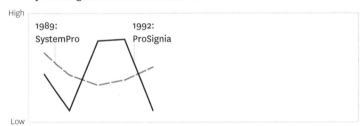

By following its first value innovation . . .

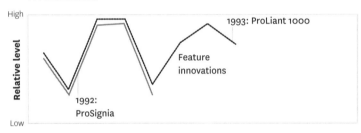

. . . with another

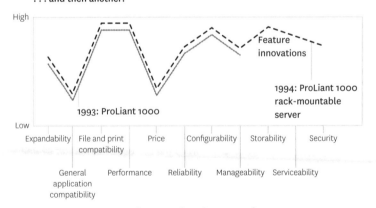

. . . and then another.

Elements of product or service

As competitors tried to imitate the ProSignia and value curves in the industry began to converge, Compaq took another leap, this time from the service platform. Viewing its servers not as stand-alone products but as elements of its customers' total computing needs, Compaq saw that 90% of customers' costs were in servicing networks and only 10% were in the server hardware itself. Yet Compaq, like other companies in the industry, had been focusing on maximizing the price/performance ratio of the server hardware, the least costly element for buyers.

Compaq redeployed its resources to bring out the ProLiant 1000, a server that incorporates two innovative pieces of software. The first, SmartStart, configures server hardware and network information to suit a company's operating system and application programs. It slashes the time it takes a customer to configure a server network and makes installation virtually error free so that servers perform reliably from day one. The second piece of software, Insight Manager, helps customers manage their server networks by, for example, spotting overheating boards or troubled disk drives before they break down.

By innovating on the service platform, Compaq created a superior value curve and expanded its market. Companies lacking expertise in information technology had been skeptical of their ability to configure and manage a network server. SmartStart and Insight Manager helped put those companies at ease. The ProLiant 1000 came out a winner.

As more and more companies acquired servers, Compaq observed that its customers often lacked the space to store the equipment properly. Stuffed into closets or left on the floor with tangled wires, expensive servers were often damaged, were certainly not secure, and were difficult to service.

By focusing on customer value—not on competitors—Compaq saw that it was time for another value innovation on the product platform. The company introduced the ProLiant 1000 rack-mountable server, which allows companies to store servers in a tall, lean cabinet in a central location. The product makes efficient use of space and ensures that machines are protected and are easy to monitor, repair, and enhance. Compaq designed the rack mount to fit both its products and those of other manufacturers, thus attracting even more buyers and discouraging imitation. The company's sales and profits rose again as its new value curve diverged from the industry's.

Compaq is now looking to the delivery platform for a value innovation that will dramatically reduce the lead time between a customer's order and the arrival of the equipment. Lead times have forced customers to forecast their needs—a difficult task—and have often required them to patch together costly solutions while waiting for their orders to be filled. Now that servers are widely used and the demands placed on them are multiplying rapidly, Compaq believes that shorter lead times will provide a quantum leap in value for customers. The company is currently working on a delivery option that will permit its products to be built to customers' specifications and shipped within 48 hours of the order. That value innovation will allow Compaq to reduce its inventory costs and minimize the accumulation of outdated stock.

By achieving value innovations on all three platforms, Compaq has been able to maintain a gap between its value curve and those of other players. Despite the pace of competition in its industry, Compaq's repeated value innovations are allowing the company to remain the number one maker of servers worldwide. Since the company's turnaround, overall sales and profits have almost quadrupled.

Driving a Company for High Growth

One of the most striking findings of our research is that despite the profound impact of a company's strategic logic, that logic is often not articulated. And because it goes unstated and unexamined, a company does not necessarily apply a consistent strategic logic across its businesses.

How can senior executives promote value innovation? First, they must identify and articulate the company's prevailing strategic logic. Then they must challenge it. They must stop and think about the industry's assumptions, the company's strategic focus, and the approaches—to customers, assets and capabilities, and product and service offerings—that are taken as given. Having reframed the company's strategic logic around value innovation, senior executives must ask the four questions that translate that thinking into a new value curve: Which of the factors that our industry takes for granted should be eliminated? Which factors should be reduced well below the industry's standard? Which should be raised well above the industry's standard? Which factors should be created that the industry has never offered? Asking the full set of questions—rather than singling out one or two—is necessary for profitable growth. Value innovation is the simultaneous pursuit of radically superior value for buyers and lower costs for companies.

For managers of diversified corporations, the logic of value innovation can be used to identify the most promising possibilities for growth across a portfolio of businesses. The value innovators we studied all have been pioneers in their industries, not necessarily in developing new technologies but in pushing the value they offer customers to new frontiers. Extending the pioneer metaphor can provide a useful way of talking about the growth potential of current and future businesses.

A company's pioneers are the businesses that offer unprecedented value. They are the most powerful sources of profitable growth. At the other extreme are settlers—businesses with value curves that conform to the basic shape of the industry's. Settlers will not generally contribute much to a company's growth. The potential of migrators lies somewhere in between. Such businesses extend the industry's curve by giving customers more for less, but they don't alter its basic shape.

A useful exercise for a management team pursuing growth is to plot the company's current and planned portfolios on a pioneer-migrator-settler map. (See the exhibit "Testing the growth potential of a portfolio of businesses.") If both the current portfolio and the planned offerings consist mainly of settlers, the company has a low growth trajectory and needs to push for value innovation. The company may well have fallen into the trap of competing. If current and planned offerings consist of a lot of migrators, reasonable growth

Testing the growth potential of a portfolio of businesses

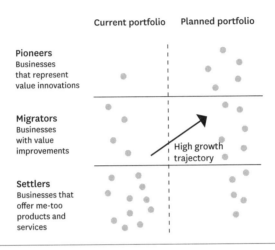

can be expected. But the company is not exploiting its potential for growth and risks being marginalized by a value innovator. This exercise is especially valuable for managers who want to see beyond today's performance numbers. Revenue, profitability, market share, and customer satisfaction are all measures of a company's current position. Contrary to what conventional strategic thinking suggests, those measures cannot point the way to the future. The pioneer-migrator-settler map can help a company predict and plan future growth and profit, a task that is especially difficult—and crucial—in a fast-changing economy.

Originally published in January–February 1997. Reprint R0407P

Fair Process

Managing in the Knowledge Economy

A LONDON POLICEMAN GAVE a woman a ticket for making an illegal turn. When the woman protested that there was no sign prohibiting the turn, the policeman pointed to one that was bent out of shape and difficult to see from the road. Furious, the woman decided to appeal by going to court. Finally, the day of her hearing arrived, and she could hardly wait to speak her piece. But she had just begun to tell her side of the story when the magistrate stopped her and summarily ruled in her favor.

How did the woman feel? Vindicated? Victorious? Satisfied?

No, she was frustrated and deeply unhappy. "I came for justice," she complained, "but the magistrate never let me explain what happened." In other words, although she liked the outcome, she didn't like the process that had created it.

For the purposes of their theories, economists assume that people are maximizers of utility, driven mainly by rational calculations of their own self-interest. That is, economists assume people focus solely on outcomes. That assumption has migrated into much of management theory and practice. It has, for instance, become embedded in the tools managers traditionally use to control and motivate employees—from incentive systems to organizational structures. But it is an assumption that managers would do well to reexamine because we all know that in real life it doesn't always hold true. People do care about outcomes, but—like the woman in London—they also care about the processes that produce those outcomes. They want to know that they had their say—that their point of view was considered even if it was rejected. Outcomes matter, but no more than the fairness of the processes that produce them.

Never has the idea of fair process been more important for managers than it is today. Fair process turns out to be a powerful management tool for companies struggling to make the transition from a production-based to a knowledge-based economy, in which value creation depends increasingly on ideas and innovation. Fair process profoundly influences attitudes and behaviors critical to high performance. It builds trust and unlocks ideas. With it, managers can achieve even the most painful and difficult goals while gaining the voluntary cooperation of the employees affected. Without fair process, even outcomes that employees might favor can be difficult to achieve—as the experience of an elevator manufacturer we'll call Elco illustrates.

Good Outcome, Unfair Process

In the late 1980s, sales in the elevator industry headed south as over-construction of office space left some large U.S. cities with vacancy rates as high as 20%. Faced with diminished domestic demand for its product, Elco knew it had to improve its operations. The company made the decision to replace its batch-manufacturing system with a cellular approach that would allow self-directed teams to achieve superior performance. Given the industry's collapse, top management felt the transformation had to be made in record time.

Lacking expertise in cellular manufacturing, Elco retained a consulting firm to design a master plan for the conversion. Elco asked the consultants to work quickly and with minimal disturbance to employees. The new manufacturing system would be installed first at Elco's Chester plant, where employee relations were so good that in 1983 workers had decertified their own union. Subsequently, Elco would roll the process out to its High Park plant, where a strong union would probably resist that, or any other, change.

Idea in Brief

In just months, a model workforce degenerated into a cauldron of mistrust, resistance, and plummeting performance. Why? Management launched a major change effort without inviting employees' input, without explaining the reasons for the change, and without clarifying new performance expectations.

In other words, the company ignored **fair process**—a decision-making approach that addresses our basic human need to be valued and respected. When people feel a decision affecting them was made fairly, they trust and cooperate with managers. They share ideas and willingly go beyond the call of duty. Corporate performance soars.

In knowledge-based organizations— whose lifeblood consists of

employees' trust, commitment, and ideas—fair process is essential. It enables companies to channel people's energy and creativity toward organizational goals.

The benefits of fair process may seem obvious—yet most organizations don't practice it. Why? Some managers find it threatening, assuming it will diminish their power. They keep employees at arm's length to avoid challenges to their authority. Others believe employees are concerned only with what's best for themselves. But evidence shows that most people will accept outcomes not wholly in their favor—*if* they believe the process for arriving at those outcomes was fair.

Under the leadership of a much beloved plant manager, Chester was in all respects a model operation. Visiting customers were always impressed by the knowledge and enthusiasm of Chester's employees, so much so that the vice president of marketing saw the plant as one of Elco's best marketing tools. "Just let customers talk with Chester employees," he observed, "and they walk away convinced that buying an Elco elevator is the smart choice."

But one day in January of 1991, Chester's employees arrived at work to discover strangers at the plant. Who were these people wearing dark suits, white dress shirts, and ties? They weren't customers. They showed up daily and spoke in low tones to one another. They didn't interact with employees. They hovered behind people's backs, taking notes and drawing fancy diagrams. The rumor circulated that after employees went home in the afternoon, these people would

Idea in Practice

Fair process isn't decision by consensus or democracy in the workplace. Its goal is to pursue the best ideas, not create harmony. Fair process consists of three principles:

- *Engagement*—involving individuals in decisions by inviting their input and encouraging them to challenge one another's ideas. Engagement communicates management's respect for individuals and their ideas and builds collective wisdom. It generates better decisions and greater commitment from those involved in executing those decisions.

- *Explanation*—clarifying the thinking behind a final decision. Explanation reassures people that managers have considered their opinions and made the decision with the company's overall interests at heart. Employees trust managers' intentions—even if their own ideas were rejected.

- *Expectation clarity*—stating the new rules of the game, including performance standards, penalties for failure, and new responsibilities. By minimizing political jockeying and favoritism, expectation clarity enables

employees to focus on the job at hand.

Example: Facing decreasing demand, an elevator manufacturer we'll call Elco decided to design a more efficient manufacturing system. It would introduce the system at its Chester plant, a model operation with such positive employee relations that it decertified its own union. Then it would incorporate the new system at High Park, a strongly unionized plant highly resistant to change.

Seeking minimal workforce disturbance, managers didn't involve the Chester employees in the system design process, explain why change was necessary, or clarify new performance expectations. Soon rumors about layoffs proliferated, trust and commitment deteriorated, and fights erupted on the shop floor. Quality sank.

Rattled but wiser, Elco took a different tack at their High Park site. Managers held ongoing plantwide meetings to explain the need for the new system, encouraged employees to help design the new process, and laid out new expectations. The anticipated resistance never came—and trusting employees embraced the new system.

swarm across the plant floor, snoop around people's workstations, and have heated discussions.

During this period, the plant manager was increasingly absent. He was spending more time at Elco's head office in meetings with the consultants—sessions deliberately scheduled away from the plant so as not to distract the employees. But the plant manager's absence produced the opposite effect. As people grew anxious, wondering why the captain of their ship seemed to be deserting them, the rumor mill moved into high gear. Everyone became convinced that the consultants would downsize the plant. They were sure they were about to lose their jobs. The fact that the plant manager was always gone—obviously, he was avoiding them—and that no explanation was given, could only mean that management was, they thought, "trying to pull one over on us." Trust and commitment at the Chester plant quickly deteriorated. Soon, people were bringing in newspaper clippings about other plants around the country that had been shut down with the help of consultants. Employees saw themselves as imminent victims of yet another management fad and resented it.

In fact, Elco managers had no intention of closing the plant. They wanted to cut out waste, freeing people to enhance quality and produce elevators for new international markets. But plant employees could not have known that.

The master plan
In March 1991, management gathered the Chester employees in a large room. Three months after the consultants had first appeared, they were formally introduced. At the same time, management unveiled to employees the master plan for change at the Chester plant. In a meeting that lasted only 30 minutes, employees heard how their time-honored way of working would be abolished and replaced by something called "cellular manufacturing." No one explained why the change was needed, nor did anyone say exactly what would be expected of employees under the new approach. The managers didn't mean to skirt the issues; they just didn't feel they had the time to go into details.

The employees sat in stunned silence, which the managers mistook for acceptance, forgetting how many months it had taken them as leaders to get comfortable with the idea of cellular manufacturing and the changes it entailed. The managers felt good when the meeting was over, believing the employees were on board. With such a terrific staff, they thought, implementation of the new system was bound to go well.

Master plan in hand, management quickly began rearranging the plant. When employees asked what the new layout aimed to achieve, the response was "efficiency gains." The managers didn't have time to explain why efficiency needed to be improved and didn't want to worry employees. But lacking an intellectual understanding of what was happening to them, some employees literally began feeling sick when they came to work.

Managers informed employees that they would no longer be judged on individual performance but rather on the performance of the cell. They said quicker or more experienced employees would have to pick up the slack for slower or less experienced colleagues. But they didn't elaborate. How the new system was supposed to work, management didn't make clear.

In fact, the new cell design offered tremendous benefits to employees, making vacations easier to schedule, for example, and giving them the opportunity to broaden their skills and engage in a greater variety of work. But lacking trust in the change process, employees could see only its negative side. They began taking out their fears and anger on one another. Fights erupted on the plant floor as employees refused to help those they called "lazy people who can't finish their own jobs" or interpreted offers of help as meddling, responding with, "This is my job. You keep to your own workstation."

Chester's model workforce was falling apart. For the first time in the plant manager's career, employees refused to do as they were asked, turning down assignments "even if you fire me." They felt they could no longer trust the once popular plant manager, so they began to go around him, taking their complaints directly to his boss at the head office.

The plant manager then announced that the new cell design would allow employees to act as self-directed teams and that the role of the supervisor would be abolished. He expected people to react with excitement to his vision of Chester as the epitome of the factory of the future, where employees are empowered as entrepreneurial agents. Instead, they were simply confused. They had no idea how to succeed in this new environment. Without supervisors, what would they do if stock ran short or machines broke down? Did empowerment mean that the teams could self-authorize overtime, address quality problems such as rework, or purchase new machine tools? Unclear about how to succeed, employees felt set up to fail.

Time out

By the summer of 1991, both cost and quality performance were in a free fall. Employees were talking about bringing the union back. Finally, in despair, the plant manager phoned Elco's industrial psychologist. "I need your help," he said. "I have lost control."

The psychologist conducted an employee opinion survey to learn what had gone wrong. Employees complained, "Management doesn't care about our ideas or our input." They felt that the company had scant respect for them as individuals, treating them as if they were not worthy of knowing about business conditions: "They don't bother to tell us where we are going and what this means to us." And they were deeply confused and mistrustful: "We don't know exactly what management expects of us in this new cell."

What Is Fair Process?

The theme of justice has preoccupied writers and philosophers throughout the ages, but the systematic study of fair process emerged only in the mid-1970s, when two social scientists, John W. Thibaut and Laurens Walker, combined their interest in the psychology of justice with the study of process. Focusing their attention on legal settings, they sought to understand what makes people trust a legal system so that they will comply with laws without being coerced into doing so. Their research established that people care as much about the fairness of the process through which an outcome is produced as they do about the outcome itself. Subsequent researchers such as Tom R. Tyler and E. Allan Lind demonstrated the power of fair process across diverse cultures and social settings.

We discovered the managerial relevance of fair process more than a decade ago, during a study of strategic decision making in multinational corporations. Many top executives in those corporations were frustrated—and baffled—by the way the senior managers of their local subsidiaries behaved. Why did those managers so often fail to share information and ideas with the executives? Why did they sabotage the execution of plans they had agreed to carry out? In the 19 companies we studied, we found a direct link between processes, attitudes, and behavior. Managers who believed the company's processes were fair displayed a high level of trust and commitment, which, in turn, engendered active cooperation. Conversely, when managers felt fair process was absent, they hoarded ideas and dragged their feet.

In subsequent field research, we explored the relevance of fair process in other business contexts—for example, in companies in the midst of transformations, in teams engaged in product innovation, and in company-supplier partnerships. (See the sidebar "Making Sense of Irrational Behavior at VW and Siemens-Nixdorf.") For companies seeking to harness the energy and creativity of committed managers and employees, the central idea that emerges from our fair-process research is this: Individuals are most likely to trust and cooperate freely with systems—whether they themselves win or lose by those systems—when fair process is observed.

Fair process responds to a basic human need. All of us, whatever our role in a company, want to be valued as human beings and not as "personnel" or "human assets." We want others to respect our intelligence. We want our ideas to be taken seriously. And we want to understand the rationale behind specific decisions. People are sensitive to the signals conveyed through a company's decision-making processes. Such processes can reveal a company's willingness to trust people and seek their ideas—or they can signal the opposite.

The three principles

In all the diverse management contexts we have studied, we have asked people to identify the bedrock elements of fair process. And whether we were working with senior executives or shop floor employees, the same three mutually reinforcing principles consistently emerged: engagement, explanation, and expectation clarity.

Engagement means involving individuals in the decisions that affect them by asking for their input and allowing them to refute the merits of one another's ideas and assumptions. Engagement communicates management's respect for individuals and their ideas. Encouraging refutation sharpens everyone's thinking and builds collective wisdom. Engagement results in better decisions by management and greater commitment from all involved in executing those decisions.

Explanation means that everyone involved and affected should understand why final decisions are made as they are. An explanation of the thinking that underlies decisions makes people confident that managers have considered their opinions and have made those decisions impartially in the overall interests of the company. An explanation allows employees to trust managers' intentions even if their own ideas have been rejected. It also serves as a powerful feedback loop that enhances learning.

Expectation clarity requires that once a decision is made, managers state clearly the new rules of the game. Although the expectations may be demanding, employees should know up front by what standards they will be judged and the penalties for failure. What are the new targets and milestones? Who is responsible for what? To achieve fair process, it matters less what the new rules and policies are and more that they are clearly understood. When people clearly understand what is expected of them, political jockeying and favoritism are minimized, and they can focus on the job at hand.

Notice that fair process is not decision by consensus. Fair process does not set out to achieve harmony or to win people's support through compromises that accommodate every individual's opinions, needs, or interests. While fair process gives every idea a chance, the merit of the ideas—and not consensus—is what drives the decision making.

Making Sense of Irrational Behavior at VW and Siemens-Nixdorf

ECONOMIC THEORIES DO A GOOD job of explaining the rational side of human behavior, but they fall short in explaining why people can act negatively in the face of positive outcomes. Fair process offers managers a theory of behavior that explains—or might help predict—what would otherwise appear to be bewilderingly noneconomic, or irrational, behavior.

Consider what happened to Volkswagen. In 1992, the German carmaker was in the midst of expanding its manufacturing facility in Puebla, Mexico, its only production site in North America. The appreciation of the deutsche mark against the U.S. dollar was pricing Volkswagen out of the U.S. market. But after the North American Free Trade Agreement (NAFTA) became law in 1992, Volkswagen's cost-efficient Mexican facility was well positioned to reconquer the large North American market.

In the summer of 1992, a new labor agreement had to be hammered out. The accord VW signed with the union's secretary-general included a generous 20% pay raise for employees. VW thought the workers would be pleased.

But the union's leaders had not involved the employees in discussions about the contract's terms; they did a poor job of communicating what the new agreement would mean to employees and why a number of work-rule changes were necessary. Workers did not understand the basis for the decisions their leaders had taken. They felt betrayed.

VW's management was completely caught off guard when, on July 21, the employees started a massive walkout that cost the company as much as an estimated $10 million per day. On August 21, about 300 protesters were attacked by police dogs. The government was forced to step in to end the violence. Volkswagen's plans for the U.S. market were in disarray, and its performance was devastated.

In contrast, consider the turnaround of Siemens-Nixdorf Informationssysteme (SNI), the largest European supplier of information technology. Created in 1990 when Siemens acquired the troubled Nixdorf Computer Company, SNI had cut head count from 52,000 to 35,000 by 1994. Anxiety and fear were rampant at the company.

In 1994, Gerhard Schulmeyer, the newly appointed CEO, went out to talk to as many employees as he could. In a series of meetings large and small with a total of more than 11,000 people, Schulmeyer shared his crusading mission to engage everyone in turning the company around. He began by painting a bleakly honest picture of SNI's situation: The company was losing money despite recent efforts to slash costs. Deeper cuts were needed, and every business would have to demonstrate its viability or be eliminated. Schulmeyer set clear but tough rules about how decisions would be made. He then asked for volunteers to come up with ideas.

Within three months, the initial group of 30 volunteers grew to encompass an additional 75 SNI executives and 300 employees. These 405 change agents soon turned into 1,000, then 3,000, then 9,000, as they progressively recruited others to help save the company. Throughout the process, ideas were solicited from managers and employees alike concerning decisions that affected them, and they all understood how decisions would be made. Ideas would be auctioned off to executives willing to champion and finance them. If no executive bought a proposal on its merits, the idea would not be pursued. Although 20% to 30% of their proposals were rejected, employees thought the process was fair.

People voluntarily pitched in—mostly after business hours, often until midnight. In just over two years, SNI has achieved a transformation notable in European corporate history. Despite accumulated losses of DM 2 billion, by 1995 SNI was already operating in the black. In the same period, employee satisfaction almost doubled, despite the radical and difficult changes under way.

Why did employees of Volkswagen revolt, despite their upbeat economic circumstances? How, in the face of such demoralizing economic conditions, could SNI turn around its performance? What is at issue is not *what* the two companies did but *how* they did it. The cases illustrate the tremendous power of fair process—fairness in the process of making and executing decisions. Fair process profoundly influences attitudes and behavior critical to high performance.

Nor is fair process the same as democracy in the workplace. Achieving fair process does not mean that managers forfeit their prerogative to make decisions and establish policies and procedures. Fair process pursues the best ideas whether they are put forth by one or many.

"We really screwed up"

Elco managers violated all three basic principles of fair process at the Chester plant. They failed to engage employees in decisions that directly affected them. They didn't explain why decisions were being made the way they were and what those decisions meant to employees' careers and work methods. And they neglected to make clear what would be expected of employees under cellular manufacturing. In the absence of fair process, the employees at Chester rejected the transformation.

A week after the psychologist's survey was completed, management invited employees to meetings in groups of 20. Employees surmised that management was either going to pretend that the survey had never happened or accuse employees of disloyalty for having voiced their complaints. But to their amazement, managers kicked off the meeting by presenting the undiluted survey results and declaring, "We were wrong. We really screwed up. In our haste and ignorance, we did not go through the proper process." Employees couldn't believe their ears. There were whispers in the back of the room, "What the devil did they say?" At more than 20 meetings over the next few weeks, managers repeated their confession. "No one was prepared to believe us at first," one manager said. "We had screwed up too badly."

At subsequent meetings, management shared with employees the company's dismal business forecast and the limited options available. Without cost reduction, Elco would have to raise its prices, and higher prices would further depress sales. That would mean cutting production even more, perhaps even moving manufacturing offshore. Heads nodded. Employees saw the bind the company was in. The business problem was becoming theirs, not just management's.

But still there were concerns: "If we help to cut costs and learn to produce elevators that are twice as good in half the time, will we work ourselves out of a job?" In response, the managers described their strategy to increase sales outside the United States. They also announced a new policy called *proaction time:* No one would be laid off because of any improvements made by an employee. Instead, employees could use their newly free time to attend cross-training programs designed to give them the skills they would need to work in any area of operations. Or employees could act as consultants addressing quality issues. In addition, management agreed not to replace any departing employees with new hires until business conditions improved. At the same time, however, management made it clear that it retained the right to let people go if business conditions grew worse.

Employees may not have liked what they heard, but they understood it. They began to see that they shared responsibility with management for Elco's success. If they could improve quality and productivity, Elco could bring more value to the market and prevent further sales erosion. To give employees confidence that they were not being misled, management pledged to regularly share data on sales, costs, and market trends—a first step toward rebuilding trust and commitment.

Elco's managers could not undo past mistakes, but they could involve employees in making future decisions. Managers asked employees why they thought the new manufacturing cells weren't working and how to fix them. Employees suggested making changes in the location of materials, in the placement of machines, and in the way tasks were performed. They began to share their knowledge; as they did so, the cells were redesigned and performance steadily improved, often far exceeding the expectations originally set by the consultants. As trust and commitment were restored, talk of bringing the union back died out.

High Park's turn
Meanwhile, management worried about introducing the new work methods at Elco's High Park plant, which, unlike the Chester plant,

had a history of resisting change. The union was strong at High Park, and some employees there had as much as 25 years' service. Moreover, the plant manager, a young engineer new to High Park, had never run a plant before. The odds seemed to be against him. If change had created animosity at Chester, one could only imagine how much worse the situation could become at High Park.

But management's fears went unrealized. When the consultants came to the plant, the young manager introduced them to all employees. At a series of plantwide meetings, corporate executives openly discussed business conditions and the company's declining sales and profits. They explained that they had visited other companies' plants and had seen the productivity improvements that cellular manufacturing could bring. They announced the proaction-time policy to calm employees' justifiable fears of layoffs. At the High Park plant, managers encouraged employees to help the consultants design the new manufacturing cells, and they encouraged active debate. Then, as the old performance measures were discarded, managers worked with employees to develop new ones and to establish the cell teams' new responsibilities.

Every day, the High Park plant manager waited for the anticipated meltdown, but it never came. Of course, there were some gripes, but even when people didn't like the decisions, they felt they had been treated fairly and, so, willingly participated in the plant's eventual performance turnaround.

Three years later, we revisited a popular local eatery to talk with people from both plants. Employees from both Chester and High Park now believe that the cellular approach is a better way to work. High Park employees spoke about their plant manager with admiration, and they commiserated with the difficulties Elco's managers had in making the changeover to cellular manufacturing. They concluded that it had been a necessary, worthwhile, and positive experience. But Chester employees spoke with anger and indignation as they described their treatment by Elco's managers. (See "The Price of Unfairness.") For them, as for the London woman who had been unfairly ticketed, fair process was as important as—if not more important than—the outcome.

The Price of Unfairness

HISTORICALLY, POLICIES DESIGNED TO ESTABLISH fair process in organizations arise mainly in reaction to employees' complaints and uprisings. But by then it is too late. When individuals have been so angered by the violation of fair process that they have been driven to organized protest, their demands often stretch well beyond the reasonable to a desire for what theorists call *retributive justice:* Not only do they want fair process restored, they also seek to visit punishment and vengeance upon those who have violated it in compensation for the disrespect the unfair process signals.

Lacking trust in management, employees push for policies that are laboriously detailed, inflexible, and often administratively constricting. They want to ensure that managers will never have the discretion to act unjustly again. In their indignation, they may try to roll back decisions imposed unfairly even when the decisions themselves were good ones—even when they were critical to the company's competitiveness or beneficial to the workers themselves. Such is the emotional power that unfair process can provoke.

Managers who view fair process as a nuisance or as a limit on their freedom to manage must understand that it is the violation of fair process that will wreak the most serious damage on corporate performance. Retribution can be very expensive.

Fair Process in the Knowledge Economy

Fair process may sound like a soft issue, but understanding its value is crucial for managers trying to adapt their companies to the demands of the knowledge-based economy. Unlike the traditional factors of production—land, labor, and capital—knowledge is a resource locked in the human mind. Creating and sharing knowledge are intangible activities that can neither be supervised nor forced out of people. They happen only when people cooperate voluntarily. As the Nobel laureate economist Friedrich Hayek has argued, "Practically every individual . . . possesses unique information" that can be put to use only with "his active cooperation." Getting that cooperation may well turn out to be one of the key managerial issues of the next few decades. (See "Fair Process Is Critical in Knowledge Work.")

Fair Process Is Critical in Knowledge Work

IT IS EASY TO SEE FAIR process at work on the plant floor, where its violation can produce such highly visible manifestations as strikes, slowdowns, and high defect rates. But fair process can have an even greater impact on the quality of professional and managerial work. That is because innovation is the key challenge of the knowledge-based economy, and innovation requires the exchange of ideas, which in turn depends on trust.

Executives and professionals rarely walk the picket line, but when their trust has not been won, they frequently withhold their full cooperation—and their ideas. In knowledge work, then, ignoring fair process creates high opportunity costs in the form of ideas that never see daylight and initiatives that are never seized. For example:

A multifunctional team is created to develop an important new product. Because it contains representatives from every major functional area of the company, the team *should* produce more innovative products, with less internal fighting, shortened lead times, and lower costs. The team meets, but people drag their feet. Executives at a computer maker developing a new workstation, for example, thoughtfully deploy the traditional management levers. They hammer out a good incentive scheme. They define the project scope and structure. And they allocate the right resources. Yet the trust, idea sharing, and commitment that everyone wants never materialize. Why? Early in the project, manufacturing and marketing representatives on the team propose building a prototype, but the strong design-engineering group driving the project ignores them. Subsequently, problems surface because the design is difficult to manufacture and the application software is inadequate. The team members from manufacturing and marketing are aware of these issues all along but remain passive in sharing their concerns with

---

Voluntary cooperation was not what Frederick Winslow Taylor had in mind when at the turn of the century he began to develop an arsenal of tools to promote efficiency and consistency by controlling individuals' behavior and compelling employees to comply with management dictates. Traditional management science, which is rooted in Taylor's time-and-motion studies, encouraged a managerial preoccupation with allocating resources, creating economic incentives and rewards, monitoring and measuring performance, and manipulating organizational structures to set lines of authority. These conventional management levers still have

the powerful design engineers. Instead, they wait until the problems reveal themselves—at which time they are very expensive to fix.

Two companies create a joint venture that offers clear benefits to both parties. But they then hold their cards so close to their chests that they ensure the alliance will create limited value for either partner. The Chinese joint-venture partner of a European engineering group, for example, withholds critical information from the field, failing to report that customers are having problems installing the partner's products and sitting on requests for new product features. Why do the Chinese fail to cooperate fully, even if it means hurting their own business?

Early in the partnership, the Chinese felt they had been shut out of key product and operating decisions. To make matters worse, the Europeans never explained the logic guiding their decisions. As the Chinese withhold critical information, the increasingly frustrated European partner responds in kind by slowing the transfer of managerial know-how, which the Chinese need badly.

Two companies create a supplier partnership to achieve improved value at lower cost. They agree to act in a seamless fashion, as one company. But the supplier seems to spend more energy on developing other customers than on deepening the partnership. One consumer goods manufacturer, for example, keeps delaying the installation of a joint electronic consumer-response data system with a major food retailer. The system will substantially improve inventory management for both partners. But the supplier remains too wary to invest. Why? The retailer has a history of dropping some of the supplier's products without explanation. And the consumer company can't understand the retailer's ambiguous criteria for designating "preferred suppliers."

their role to play, but they have little to do with encouraging active cooperation. Instead, they operate in the realm of outcome fairness or what social scientists call *distributive justice,* where the psychology works like this: When people get the compensation (or the resources, or the place in the organizational hierarchy) they deserve, they feel satisfied with that outcome. They will reciprocate by fulfilling to the letter their obligation to the company. The psychology of fair process, or *procedural justice,* is quite different. Fair process builds trust and commitment, trust and commitment produce voluntary cooperation, and voluntary cooperation drives performance, leading people to go beyond the call of duty by sharing their knowledge and applying their creativity. In all the management contexts we've studied, whatever the task, we have consistently observed this dynamic at work. (See the exhibit "Two complementary paths to performance.")

Consider the transformation of Bethlehem Steel Corporation's Sparrows Point, Maryland, division, a business unit responsible for marketing, sales, production, and financial performance. Until 1993, the 106-year-old division was managed in the classic command-and-control style. People were expected to do what they were told to do—no more and no less—and management and employees saw themselves as adversaries.

That year, Bethlehem Steel introduced a management model so different at Sparrows Point that Taylor—who was, in fact, the company's consulting engineer about 100 years ago—wouldn't have recognized it. The new model was designed to invoke in employees an active sense of responsibility for sharing their knowledge and ideas with one another and with management. It was also meant to encourage them to take the initiative for getting things done. In the words of Joe Rosel, the president of one of the division's five unions, "It's all about involvement, justification for decisions, and a clear set of expectations."

At Sparrows Point, employees are involved in making and executing decisions at three levels. At the top is a joint-leadership team, composed of senior managers and five employee representatives, that deals with companywide issues when they arise. At the department level are area teams, consisting of managers like superintendents and of employees from the different areas of the plant, such as zone committee people. Those teams deal with day-to-day operational issues such as customer service, quality, and logistics. Ad hoc problem-solving teams of employees address opportunities and obstacles as they arise on the shop floor. At each level, teammates share and debate their ideas. Thus, employees are assured a fair hearing for their points of view on decisions likely to affect them. With the exception of decisions involving major changes or resource commitments, the teams make and execute the decisions themselves.

Two complementary paths to performance

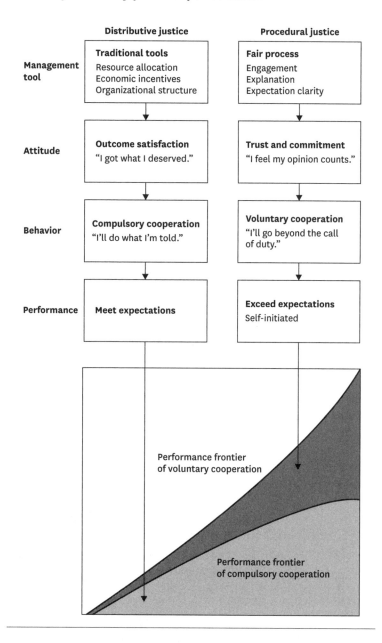

	Distributive justice	**Procedural justice**
Management tool	**Traditional tools** Resource allocation Economic incentives Organizational structure	**Fair process** Engagement Explanation Expectation clarity
Attitude	**Outcome satisfaction** "I got what I deserved."	**Trust and commitment** "I feel my opinion counts."
Behavior	**Compulsory cooperation** "I'll do what I'm told."	**Voluntary cooperation** "I'll go beyond the call of duty."
Performance	**Meet expectations**	**Exceed expectations** Self-initiated

Performance frontier
of voluntary cooperation

Performance frontier
of compulsory cooperation

Sparrows Point uses numerous processes and devices to ensure that all employees can understand why decisions have been made and how such decisions need to be executed. There is, for example, a bulletin board where decisions are posted and explained, allowing employees who haven't been directly involved in those decisions to understand what's going on and why. In addition, in more than 70 four-hour seminars, groups ranging in size from 50 to 250 employees have met to discuss changes occurring at the division, learn about new ideas under consideration, and find out how changes might affect employees' roles and responsibilities. A quarterly newsletter and a monthly "report card" of the division's strategic, marketing, operational, and financial performance keeps each of the unit's 5,300 employees informed. And the teams report back to their colleagues about the changes they are making, seeking help in making the ideas work.

Fair process has produced significant changes in people's attitudes and behavior. Consider, for example, the tin mill unit at Sparrows Point. In 1992, the unit's performance was among the worst in the industry. But then, as one employee explains, "People started coming forward and sharing their ideas. They started caring about doing great work, not just getting by. Take the success we've had in light-gauge cable sheathing. We had let this high value-added product slip because the long throughput time required for production held up the other mills in the unit. But after we started getting everyone involved and explained why we needed to improve throughput, ideas started to flow. At first, the company was doubtful: If the product had created a bottleneck before, why should it be different now? But people came up with the idea of using two sequential mills instead of one to eliminate the bottleneck. Did people suddenly get smarter? No. I'd say they started to care."

The object in creating this new way of working at Sparrows Point was to improve the intellectual buy-in and emotional commitment of employees. It has apparently been successful. Since 1993, Sparrows Point has turned a profit three years in a row, the first time that has happened since the late 1970s. The division is becoming a showcase demonstrating how a declining industry can be revitalized in today's knowledge economy. In the words of one Sparrows Point employee, "Since we know now everything that's going on in the company, we have more trust in management and are more committed to making things happen. People have started doing things beyond the normal call of duty."

Overcoming Mental Barriers

If fair process is such a simple idea and yet so powerful, why do so few companies practice it? Most people think of themselves as fair, and managers are no exception. But if you ask them what it means to be a fair manager, most will describe how they give people the authority they deserve, or the resources they need, or the rewards they have earned. In other words, they will confuse fair process with fair outcomes. The few managers who focus on process might identify only one of the three fair-process principles (the most widely understood is engagement), and they would stop there.

But there are two more fundamental reasons, beyond this simple lack of understanding, that explain why fair process is so rare. The first involves power. Some managers continue to believe that knowledge is power and that they retain power only by keeping what they know to themselves. Their implicit strategy is to preserve their managerial discretion by deliberately leaving the rules for success and failure vague. Other managers maintain control by keeping employees at arm's length, substituting memos and forms for direct, two-way communication, thus avoiding challenges to their ideas or authority. Such styles can reflect deeply ingrained patterns of behavior, and rarely are managers conscious of how they exercise power. For them, fair process would represent a threat.

The second reason is also largely unconscious because it resides in an economic assumption that most of us have grown up taking at face value: the belief that people are concerned only with what's best for themselves. But, as we have seen, there is ample evidence to show that when the process is perceived to be fair, most people will accept outcomes that are not wholly in their favor. People realize that compromises and sacrifices are necessary on the job. They accept the need for short-term personal sacrifices in order to advance the long-term interests of the corporation. Acceptance is conditional, however, hinged as it is on fair process.

Fair process reaches into a dimension of human psychology that hasn't been fully explored in conventional management practice. Yet every company can tap into the voluntary cooperation of its people by building trust through fair processes.

Originally published in July–August 1997. Reprint R0301K

Creating New
Market Space

COMPETING HEAD-TO-HEAD CAN BE CUTTHROAT, especially when markets are flat or growing slowly. Managers caught in this kind of competition almost universally say they dislike it and wish they could find a better alternative. They often know instinctively that innovation is the only way they can break free from the pack. But they simply don't know where to begin. Admonitions to develop more creative strategies or to think outside the box are rarely accompanied by practical advice.

For almost a decade, we have researched companies that have created such fundamentally new and superior value. We have looked for patterns in the way companies create new markets and re-create existing ones, and we have found six basic approaches. All come from looking at familiar data from a new perspective; none requires any special vision or foresight about the future.

Most companies focus on matching and beating their rivals, and as a result their strategies tend to converge along the same basic dimensions of competition. Such companies share an implicit set of beliefs about "how we compete in our industry or in our strategic group." They share a conventional wisdom about who their customers are and what they value, and about the scope of products and services their industry should be offering. The more that companies share this conventional wisdom about how they compete, the greater the competitive convergence. As rivals try to outdo one another, they end up competing solely on the basis of incremental improvements in cost or quality or both.

Creating new market space requires a different pattern of strategic thinking. Instead of looking within the accepted boundaries that define how we compete, managers can look systematically across them. By doing so, they can find unoccupied territory that represents a real breakthrough in value. This article will describe how companies can systematically pursue value innovation by looking across the conventionally defined boundaries of competition—across substitute industries, across strategic groups, across buyer groups, across complementary product and service offerings, across the functional-emotional orientation of an industry, and even across time.

Looking Across Substitute Industries

In the broadest sense, a company competes not only with the companies in its own industry but also with companies in those other industries that produce substitute products or services. In making every purchase decision, buyers implicitly weigh substitutes, often unconsciously. Going into town for dinner and a show? At some level, you've probably decided whether to drive, take the train, or call a taxi. The thought process is intuitive for individual consumers and industrial buyers alike.

For some reason, however, we often abandon this intuitive thinking when we become sellers. Rarely do sellers think consciously about how their customers make trade-offs across substitute industries. A shift in price, a change in model, even a new ad campaign can elicit a tremendous response from rivals within an industry, but the same actions in a substitute industry usually go unnoticed. Trade journals, trade shows, and consumer rating reports reinforce the vertical walls that stand between one industry and another. Often, however, the space between substitute industries provides opportunities for value innovation.

Consider Home Depot, the company that has revolutionized the do-it-yourself market in North America. In 20 years, Home Depot has become a $24 billion business, creating over 130,000 new jobs in more than 660 stores. By the end of the year 2000, the company expects to have over 1,100 stores in the Americas. Home Depot did

Idea in Brief

When the market in which you compete gets overcrowded, innovating is the only way to break free from the pack. But how do you begin? Consider **value innovation**—a strategic concept Kim and Mauborgne introduced in their 1997 *Harvard Business Review* article. Value innovators create products or services for which there are no direct competitors—and use those offerings to stake out and dominate new market spaces. They don't possess special vision or prescience; rather, they look across the conventional boundaries of competition for opportunities to provide breakthrough value for customers.

Take Intuit. In 1984, the software company looked beyond its own industry to identify choices available to consumers seeking to manage their personal finances. Buyers' options? The computer, for which costly, complicated financial management software was available—or the lowly pencil, which didn't simplify things or save time but was cheap and easy to use. Intuit created a third option: the astoundingly successful Quicken software. With its user-friendly interface, basic functions, and affordable price, Quicken leverages the computer's advantages (speed and accuracy) *and* the pencil's advantages (simplicity of use and affordability).

Operating in markets that initially have no rivals, value innovators enjoy steep growth. Consider Starbucks, which transformed a functional product (coffee) into an emotional one with its chain of "caffeine-induced oases" offering chic gathering places, relaxation, and creative coffee drinks. Starbucks enjoys margins roughly five times the industry average.

not achieve that level of growth simply by taking market share away from other hardware stores; rather, it has created a new market of do-it-yourselfers out of ordinary home owners.

There are many explanations for Home Depot's success: its warehouse format, its relatively low-cost store locations, its knowledgeable service, its combination of large stores and low prices generating high volumes and economies of scale. But such explanations miss the more fundamental question: Where did Home Depot get its original insight into how to revolutionize and expand its market?

Home Depot looked at the existing industries serving home improvement needs. It saw that people had two choices: they could

Idea in Practice

To spot additional value innovation opportunities, consider these approaches:

Look across strategic groups. Strategic groups are clusters of companies within an industry that all pursue a similar strategy, such as offering low prices or a glamorous image for consumers. Most companies try to enhance their competitive position *within* a strategic group. To create a new market space, identify factors that determine buyers' decisions to trade up or down from one group to another.

> *Example:* Sony created a whole new market: personal portable stereos. Its Walkman combined the virtues of products created by two strategic groups: manufacturers of boom boxes, characterized by great acoustics and "cool" image, and makers of transistor radios, valued for their low prices and convenient size and weight. The Walkman grabbed market share from the two strategic groups, and attracted new groups of customers, such as joggers and commuters.

Look across the chain of buyers. Instead of targeting a single obvious customer group, target other customers involved in the buying decision. Overlooked buyer groups value different features than target customers, suggesting fresh innovation opportunities.

> *Example:* While other on-line financial-information providers served brokerage IT managers, Bloomberg began serving traders and analysts. Bloomberg designed a system to offer these neglected buyers tools for accessing and immediately acting on financial information. The system included keyboards labeled with familiar financial terms, press-of-a-button analytic capability, and dual monitors for multitasking. The system also improved the quality of traders' personal lives—providing purchasing services that enabled overworked traders to buy flowers, clothing, and jewelry during trading lulls that occurred during the workday.

Look across complementary products and services. Seek untapped value hidden in other industries' offerings that affect *your* offerings' value. Define the total solution buyers seek when choosing a product or service—including what they do before, during, and after using your product.

> *Example:* With their blockbuster superstores, Borders Books & Music and Barnes & Noble transformed their product from *books* to *the pleasure of reading.* Coffee bars, wide aisles, and comfy armchairs invite people to linger. Book-savvy staff help customers make selections. And late-night closing times provide evenings of quiet reading away from harried home fronts.

hire contractors, or they could buy tools and materials from a hardware store and do the work themselves. The key to Home Depot's original insight was understanding why buyers would choose one substitute over another. (It is essential here to keep the analysis at the industry, and not the company, level.)

Why do people hire a contractor? Surely not because they value having a stranger in their house who will charge them top dollar. Surely not because they enjoy taking time off from work to wait for the contractor to show up. In fact, professional contractors have only one decisive advantage: they have specialized know-how that the home owner lacks.

So executives at Home Depot have made it their mission to bolster the competence and confidence of customers whose expertise in home repair is limited. They recruit sales assistants with significant trade experience, often former carpenters or painters. These assistants are trained to walk customers through any project—installing kitchen cabinets, for example, or building a deck. In addition, Home Depot sponsors in-store clinics that teach customers such skills as electrical wiring, carpentry, and plumbing.

To understand the rest of the Home Depot formula, now consider the flip side: Why do people choose hardware stores over professional contractors? The most common answer would be to save money. Most people can do without the features that add cost to the typical hardware store. They don't need the city locations, the neighborly service, or the nice display shelves. So Home Depot has eliminated those costly features, employing a self-service warehouse format that lowers overhead and maintenance costs, generates economies of scale in purchasing, and minimizes stock-outs.

Essentially, Home Depot offers the expertise of professional home contractors at markedly lower prices than hardware stores. By delivering the decisive advantages of both substitute industries—and eliminating or reducing everything else—Home Depot has transformed enormous latent demand for home improvement into real demand.

Intuit, the company that changed the way individuals and small businesses manage their finances, also got its insight into value

Creating a new value curve

The value curve—a graphic depiction of the way a company or an industry configures its offering to customers—is a powerful tool for creating new market space. It is drawn by plotting the performance of the offering relative to other alternatives along the key success factors that define competition in the industry or category.

To identify those alternatives, Intuit, for example, looked within its own industry—software to manage personal finances—and it also looked across substitute products to understand why customers chose one over the other. The dominant substitute for software was the lowly pencil. The value curves for these two alternatives map out the existing competitive space.

The value curves in personal finance before Quicken

The software offered relatively high levels of speed and accuracy. But customers often chose the pencil because of its advantages in price and ease of use, and most customers never used the software's optional features, which added cost and complexity to the product.

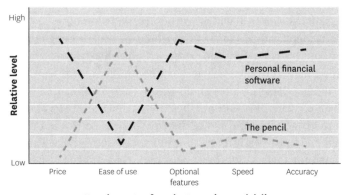

Key elements of product, service, and delivery

The key to discovering a new value curve lies in asking four basic questions:

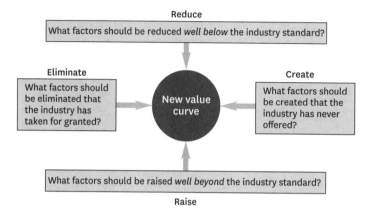

Reduce

What factors should be reduced *well below* the industry standard?

Eliminate

What factors should be eliminated that the industry has taken for granted?

New value curve

Create

What factors should be created that the industry has never offered?

What factors should be raised *well beyond* the industry standard?

Raise

Quicken's value curve

Answering the four questions led Intuit to create a new value curve, which combines the low price and ease of use of the pencil with the speed and accuracy of traditional personal-financial software.

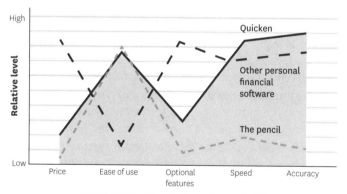

Quicken

Other personal financial software

The pencil

High

Low

Relative level

Price | Ease of use | Optional features | Speed | Accuracy

Key elements of product, service, and delivery

innovation by thinking about how customers make trade-offs across substitutes. Its Quicken software allows individuals to organize, understand, and manage their personal finances. Every household goes through the monthly drudgery of paying bills. Hence, in principle, personal financial software should be a big and broad market. Yet before Quicken, few people used software to automate this tedious and repetitive task. At the time of Quicken's release in 1984, the 42 existing software packages for personal finance had yet to crack the market.

Why? As Intuit founder Scott Cook recalls, "The greatest competitor we saw was not in the industry. It was the pencil. The pencil is a really tough and resilient substitute. Yet the entire industry had overlooked it."

Asking why buyers trade across substitutes led Intuit to an important insight: the pencil had two decisive advantages over computerized solutions—amazingly low cost and extreme simplicity of use. At prices of around $300, existing software packages were too expensive. They were also hard to use, presenting intimidating interfaces full of accounting terminology.

Intuit focused on bringing out both the decisive advantages that the computer has over the pencil—speed and accuracy—and the decisive advantages that the pencil has over computers—simplicity of use and low price—and eliminated or reduced everything else. With its user-friendly interface that resembles the familiar checkbook, Quicken is far faster and more accurate than the pencil, yet almost as simple to use. Intuit eliminated the accounting jargon and all the sophisticated features that were part of the industry's conventional wisdom about "how we compete." It offered instead only the few basic functions that most customers use. Simplifying the software cut costs. Quicken retailed at about $90, a 70% price drop. Neither the pencil nor other software packages could compete with Quicken's divergent value curve. Quicken created breakthrough value and re-created the industry, and has expanded the market some 100-fold. (See the exhibit "Creating a new value curve.")

There is a further lesson to be drawn from the way Intuit thought about and looked across substitutes. In looking for other products or services that could perform the same function as its own, Intuit could have focused on private accounting firms that handle finances for individuals. But when there is more than one substitute, it is smart to explore the ones with the greatest volumes in usage as well as in dollar value. Framed that way, more Americans use pencils than accountants to manage their personal finances.

Many of the well-known success stories of the past decade have followed this path of looking across substitutes to create new markets. Consider Federal Express and United Parcel Service, which deliver mail at close to the speed of the telephone, and Southwest Airlines, which combines the speed of flying with the convenience of frequent departures and the low cost of driving. Note that Southwest Airlines concentrated on driving as the relevant substitute, not other surface transportation such as buses, because only a minority of Americans travels long distances by bus.

Looking Across Strategic Groups Within Industries

Just as new market space often can be found by looking across substitute industries, so can it be found by looking across *strategic groups*. The term refers to a group of companies within an industry that pursue a similar strategy. In most industries, all the fundamental strategic differences among industry players are captured by a small number of strategic groups.

Strategic groups can generally be ranked in a rough hierarchical order built on two dimensions, price and performance. Each jump in price tends to bring a corresponding jump in some dimension of performance. Most companies focus on improving their competitive position *within* a strategic group. The key to creating new market space across existing strategic groups is to understand what factors determine buyers' decisions to trade up or down from one group to another.

Consider Polo Ralph Lauren, which created an entirely new and paradoxical market in clothing: high fashion with no fashion. With worldwide retail sales exceeding $5 billion, Ralph Lauren is the first American design house to successfully take its brand worldwide.

At Polo Ralph Lauren's inception more than 30 years ago, fashion industry experts of almost every stripe criticized the company. Where, they asked, was the fashion? Lacking creativity in design, how could Ralph Lauren charge such high prices? Yet the same people who criticized the company bought its clothes, as did affluent people everywhere. Lauren's lack of fashion was its greatest strength. Ralph Lauren built on the decisive advantages of the two strategic groups that dominated the high-end clothing market—designer haute couture and the higher-volume, but lower-priced, classical lines of Burberry's, Brooks Brothers, Aquascutum, and the like.

What makes people trade either up or down between haute couture and the classic lines? Most customers don't trade up to haute couture to get frivolous fashions that are rapidly outdated. Nor do they enjoy paying ridiculous prices that can reach $500 for a T-shirt. They buy haute couture for the emotional value of wearing an exclusive designer's name, a name that says, "I am different; I appreciate the finer things in life." They also value the wonderfully luxurious feel of the materials and the fine craftsmanship of the garments.

The trendy designs the fashion houses work so hard to create are, ironically, the major drawback of haute couture for most high-end customers, few of whom have the sophistication or the bodies to wear such original clothing. Conversely, customers who trade down for classic lines over haute couture want to buy garments of lasting quality that justifies high prices.

Ralph Lauren has built its brand in the space between these two strategic groups, but it didn't do so by taking the average of the groups' differences. Instead, Lauren captured the advantages of trading both up and down. Its designer name, the elegance of its stores, and the luxury of its materials capture what most customers value in haute couture; its updated classical look and price capture the best of the classical lines. By combining the most attractive factors of both groups, and eliminating or reducing everything else, Polo Ralph Lauren not only captured share from both segments but also drew many new customers into the market.

Many companies have found new market space by looking across strategic groups. In the luxury car market, Toyota's Lexus carved out a new space by offering the quality of the high-end Mercedes, BMW, and Jaguar at a price closer to the lower-end Cadillac and Lincoln. And think of the Sony Walkman. By combining the acoustics and the "cool" image of boom boxes with the low price and the convenient size and weight of transistor radios, Sony created the personal portable-stereo market in the late 1970s. The Walkman took share from these two strategic groups. In addition, its quantum leap in value drew into the market new customers like joggers and commuters.

Michigan-based Champion Enterprises found a similar opportunity by looking across two strategic groups in the housing industry: makers of prefabricated housing and on-site developers. Prefabricated houses are cheap and quick to build, but they are also dismally standardized and project an image of low quality. Houses built by developers on-site offer variety and an image of high quality but are dramatically more expensive and take longer to build.

Champion created new market space by offering the decisive advantages of both strategic groups. Its prefabricated houses are quick to build and benefit from tremendous economies of scale and lower costs, but Champion also allows buyers to choose such high-end options as fireplaces, skylights, and even vaulted ceilings. In essence, Champion has changed the definition of prefabricated housing. As a result, far more lower-to-middle-income consumers have become interested in purchasing prefabricated housing rather than renting or buying an apartment, and even some affluent people are being drawn into the market.

Looking Across the Chain of Buyers

In most industries, competitors converge around a common definition of who the target customer is when in reality there is a chain of "customers" who are directly or indirectly involved in the buying decision. The *purchasers* who pay for the product or service may differ from the actual *users*, and in some cases there are important *influencers*, as well. While these three groups may overlap, they often differ.

When they do, they frequently hold different definitions of value. A corporate purchasing agent, for example, may be more concerned with costs than the corporate user, who is likely to be far more concerned with ease of use. Likewise, a retailer may value a manufacturer's just-in-time stock-replenishment and innovative financing. But consumer purchasers, although strongly influenced by the channel, do not value these things.

Individual companies in an industry often target different customer segments—large versus small customers, for example. But an industry typically converges on a single buyer group. The pharmaceutical industry, for example, focuses overridingly on influencers—the doctors. The office equipment industry focuses heavily on purchasers—corporate purchasing departments. And the clothing industry sells predominantly to users. Sometimes there is a strong economic rationale for this focus. But often it is the result of industry practices that have never been questioned.

Challenging an industry's conventional wisdom about which buyer group to target can lead to the discovery of new market space. By looking across buyer groups, companies can gain new insights into how to redesign their value curves to focus on a previously overlooked set of customers.

Consider Bloomberg. In little over a decade, Bloomberg has become one of the largest and most profitable business-information providers in the world. Until Bloomberg's debut in the early 1980s, Reuters and Telerate dominated the on-line financial-information industry, providing news and prices in real time to the brokerage and investment community. The industry focused on purchasers—the IT managers—who valued standardized systems, which made their lives easier.

This made no sense to Bloomberg. Traders and analysts, not IT managers, make or lose millions of dollars for their employers each day. Profit opportunities come from disparities in information. When markets are active, traders and analysts must make rapid decisions. Every second counts.

So Bloomberg designed a system specifically to offer traders better value, one with easy-to-use terminals and keyboards labeled with familiar financial terms. The systems also have two flat-panel monitors, so traders can see all the information they need at once without having to open and close numerous windows. Since traders have to analyze information before they act, Bloomberg added a built-in analytic capability that works with the press of a button. Before, traders and analysts had to download data and use a pencil and calculator to perform important financial calculations. Now users can quickly run "what if" scenarios to compute returns on alternative investments, and they can perform longitudinal analyses of historical data.

By focusing on users, Bloomberg was also able to see the paradox of traders' and analysts' personal lives. They have tremendous income but work such long hours that they have little time to spend it. Realizing that markets have slow times during the day when little trading takes place, Bloomberg decided to add information and purchasing services aimed at enhancing traders' personal lives. Traders can buy items like flowers, clothing, and jewelry; make travel arrangements; get information about wines; or search through real estate listings.

By shifting its focus upstream from purchasers to users, Bloomberg created a value curve that was radically different from anything the industry had ever seen. The traders and analysts wielded their power within their firms to force IT managers to purchase Bloomberg terminals. Bloomberg did not simply win customers away from competitors—it grew the market. "We are in a business that need not be either-or," explains founder Mike Bloomberg. "Our customers can afford to have two products. Many of them take other financial news services and us because we offer uncommon value." (See the graph "Bloomberg's value curve at its debut.")

Philips Lighting Company, the North American division of the Dutch company Philips Electronics, re-created its industrial lighting business by shifting downstream from purchasers to influencers. Traditionally, the industry focused on corporate purchasing managers who bought on the basis of how much the lightbulbs cost and how long they lasted. Everyone in the industry competed head-to-head along those two dimensions.

By focusing on influencers, including CFOs and public relations people, Philips came to understand that the price and life of bulbs

Bloomberg's value curve at its debut

To establish its value curve, Bloomberg looked across the chain of buyers from the IT managers that had traditionally purchased financial information systems to the traders who used them. Its value innovation stemmed from a combination of creating new features—such as on-line analytic capabilities—that traders rather than IT managers value and raising ease of use by an order of magnitude.

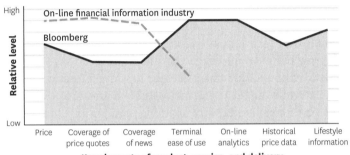

did not account for the full cost of lighting. Because lamps contained environmentally toxic mercury, companies faced high disposal costs at the end of a lamp's life. The purchasing department never saw those costs, but CFOs did. So in 1995, Philips introduced the Alto, an environmentally friendly bulb that it promotes to CFOs and to public relations people, using those influencers to drive sales. The Alto reduced customers' overall costs and garnered companies positive press for promoting environmental concerns. The new market Alto created has superior margins and is growing rapidly; the product has already replaced more than 25% of traditional T-12 fluorescent lamps used in stores, schools, and office buildings in the United States.

Many industries afford similar opportunities to create new market space. By questioning conventional definitions of who can and should be the target customer, companies can often see fundamentally new ways to create value.

Looking Across Complementary Product and Service Offerings

Few products and services are used in a vacuum; in most cases, other products and services affect their value. But in most industries, rivals converge within the bounds of their industry's product and service offerings. Take movie theaters as an example. The ease and cost of getting a babysitter and parking the car affect the perceived value of going to the movies, although these complementary services are beyond the bounds of the movie theater industry as it has been traditionally defined. Few cinema operators worry about how hard or costly it is for people to get babysitters. But they should, because it affects demand for their business.

Untapped value is often hidden in complementary products and services. The key is to define the total solution buyers seek when they choose a product or service. A simple way to do so is to think about what happens before, during, and after your product is used. Babysitting and parking the car are needed before going to the movies. Operating and application software are used along with computer hardware. In the airline industry, ground transportation is used after the flight but is clearly part of what the customer needs to travel from one place to another.

Companies can create new market space by zeroing in on the complements that detract from the value of their own product or service. Look at Borders Books & Music and Barnes & Noble in the United States. By the late 1980s, the U.S. retail-book industry appeared to be in decline. Americans were reading less and less. The large chains of mall bookstores were engaged in intense competition, and the small, independent bookstore appeared to be an endangered species.

Against this backdrop, Borders and B&N created a new format—book superstores—and woke up an entire industry. When either company enters a market, the overall consumption of books often increases by more than 50%.

The traditional business of a bookstore had been narrowly defined as selling books. People came, they bought, they left. Borders and B&N, however, thought more broadly about the total experience people seek when they buy books—and what they focused on was the joy of lifelong learning and discovery. Yes, that involves the physical purchase of books. But it also includes related activities: searching and hunting, evaluating potential purchases, and actually sampling books.

Traditional retail-book chains imposed tremendous inefficiencies and inconveniences on consumers. Their staffs were generally trained as cashiers and stock clerks; few could help customers find the right book. In small stores, selection was limited, frustrating the search for an exciting title. People who hadn't read a good book review recently or picked up a recommendation from a friend would be unlikely to patronize these bookstores. As a rule, the stores discouraged browsing, forcing customers to assume a large part of the risk in buying a book, since people would not know until after they bought it whether they would like it. As for consumption, that activity was supposed to occur at home. But as people's lives have become increasingly harried, home has become less likely to be a peaceful oasis where a person can enjoy a wonderful book.

Borders and B&N saw value trapped in these complementary activities. They hired staff with extensive knowledge of books to help customers make selections. Many staff members have college or even advanced degrees, and all are passionate book lovers. Furthermore, they're given a monthly book allowance, and they're actually encouraged to read whenever business is slow.

The superstores stock more than 150,000 titles, whereas the average bookstore contains around 20,000. The superstores are furnished with armchairs, reading tables, and sofas to encourage people not just to dip into a book or two but to read them through. Their coffee bars, classical music, and wide aisles invite people to linger comfortably. They stay open until 11 at night, offering a relaxing destination for an evening of quiet reading, not a quick shopping stop. (See the graph "Value Innovation in Book Retailing.")

Book superstores redefined the scope of the service they offer. They transformed the product from the book itself into the plea-

Value innovation in book retailing

Borders and Barnes & Noble looked across complementary products and services to establish a new value curve in book retailing. Their book superstores raised the selection of books, the level of staff knowledge, and the range of store hours well above the industry standards while lowering price and creating a wholly new reading environment.

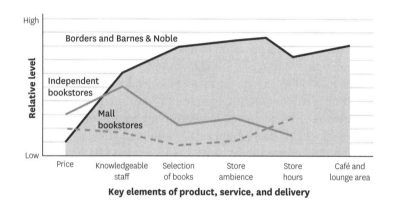

sure of reading and intellectual exploration. In less than six years, Borders and B&N have emerged as the two largest bookstore chains in the United States, with a total of more than 650 superstores between them.

We could cite many other examples of companies that have followed this path to creating new market space. Virgin Entertainment's stores combine CDs, videos, computer games, and stereo and audio equipment to satisfy buyers' complete entertainment needs. Dyson designs its vacuum cleaners to obliterate the costly and annoying activities of buying and changing vacuum cleaner bags. Zeneca's Salick cancer centers combine all the cancer treatments their patients might need under one roof so they don't have to go from one specialized center to another, making separate appointments for each service they require.

Looking Across Functional or Emotional Appeal to Buyers

Competition in an industry tends to converge not only around an accepted notion of the scope of its products and services but also around one of two possible bases of appeal. Some industries compete principally on price and function based largely on calculations of utility; their appeal is rational. Other industries compete largely on feelings; their appeal is emotional.

Yet the appeal of most products or services is rarely intrinsically one or the other. The phenomenon is a result of the way companies have competed in the past, which has unconsciously educated consumers on what to expect. Companies' behavior affects customers' expectations in a reinforcing cycle. Over time, functionally oriented industries become more functionally oriented; emotionally oriented industries become more emotionally oriented. No wonder market research rarely reveals new insights into what customers really want. Industries have trained customers in what to expect. When surveyed, they echo back: more of the same for less.

Companies often find new market space when they are willing to challenge the functional-emotional orientation of their industry. We have observed two common patterns. Emotionally oriented industries offer many extras that add price without enhancing functionality. Stripping those extras away may create a fundamentally simpler, lower-priced, lower-cost business model that customers would welcome. Conversely, functionally oriented industries can often infuse commodity products with new life by adding a dose of emotion—and in so doing, can stimulate new demand.

Look at how Starbucks transformed a functional product into an emotional one. In the late 1980s, General Foods, Nestlé, and Procter & Gamble dominated the U.S. coffee market. Consumers drank coffee as part of a daily routine. Coffee was considered a commodity industry, marked by heavy price-cutting and an ongoing battle for market share. The industry had taught customers to shop based on price, discount coupons, and brand names that are expensive for companies to build. The result was paper-thin profit margins and low growth.

Instead of viewing coffee as a functional product, Starbucks set out to make coffee an emotional experience, what customers often refer to as a "caffeine-induced oasis." The big three sold a commodity—coffee by the can; Starbucks sold a retailing concept—the coffee bar. The coffee bars offered a chic gathering place, status, relaxation, conversation, and creative coffee drinks. Starbucks turned coffee into an emotional experience and ordinary people into coffee connoisseurs for whom the steep $3-per-cup price seemed reasonable. With almost no advertising, Starbucks became a national brand with margins roughly five times the industry average.

What Starbucks did for coffee, Swatch did for budget watches. Long considered a functional item, budget watches were bought merely to keep track of time. Citizen and Seiko, the leaders in the industry, competed through advances in functionality by using quartz technology to improve accuracy, for example, or by making digital displays that were easier to read. Swatch turned budget watches into fashion accessories.

SMH, the Swiss parent company, created a design lab in Italy to turn its watches into a fashion statement, combining powerful technology with fantasy. "You wear a watch on your wrist, right against your skin," explains chairman Nicholas Hayek. "It can be an important part of your image. I believed that if we could add genuine emotion to the product and a strong message, we could succeed in dominating the industry and creating a powerful market." Before Swatch, people usually purchased only one watch. Swatch made repeat purchases the standard. In Italy, the average person owns six Swatches to fit their different moods and looks.

The Body Shop created new market space by shifting in the opposite direction, from an emotional appeal to a functional one. Few industries are more emotionally oriented than cosmetics. The industry sells glamour and beauty, hopes and dreams as much as it sells products. On average, packaging and advertising constitute 85% of cosmetics companies' costs.

By stripping away the emotional appeal, the Body Shop realized tremendous cost savings. Since customers get no practical value from the money the industry spends on packaging, the Body Shop uses simple refillable plastic bottles. The Body Shop spends little on advertising, again because its customers get no functional value from it. In short, the Body Shop hardly looks like a cosmetics company at all. The company's approach—and its emphasis on natural ingredients and healthy living—was so refreshingly simple that it won consumers over through common sense and created new market space in an industry accustomed to competing on a tried-and-true formula. (See the graph "Is the Body Shop a cosmetics company?")

A burst of new market creation is under way in a number of service industries that are following this pattern. Relationship businesses like insurance, banking, and investing have relied heavily on the emotional bond between broker and client. They are ripe for change. Direct Line Insurance in Britain, for example,

Is the Body Shop a cosmetics company?

By reconsidering the traditional basis of appeal of its industry, the Body Shop created a value curve so divergent that it hardly looks like a cosmetics company at all. In appealing to function rather than emotion, the Body Shop reduced price, glamour, and packaging costs while creating a new emphasis on natural ingredients and healthy living.

has done away with traditional brokers. It reasoned that customers would not need the hand-holding and emotional comfort that brokers traditionally provide if the company did a better job of, for example, paying claims rapidly and eliminating complicated paperwork. So instead of using brokers and regional branch offices, Direct Line substitutes information technology to improve claims handling, and it passes on some of the cost savings to customers in the form of lower insurance premiums. In the United States, Vanguard Group in index funds and Charles Schwab in brokerage services are doing the same in the investment industry, creating new market space by transforming emotionally oriented businesses based on personal relationships into high-performance, low-cost functional businesses.

Looking Across Time

All industries are subject to external trends that affect their businesses over time. Think of the rapid rise of the Internet or the global movement toward protecting the environment. Looking at these trends with the right perspective can unlock innovation that creates new market space.

Most companies adapt incrementally and somewhat passively as events unfold. Whether it's the emergence of new technologies or major regulatory changes, managers tend to focus on projecting the trend itself. That is, they ask in which direction a technology will evolve, how it will be adopted, whether it will become scalable. They pace their own actions to keep up with the development of the trends they're tracking.

But key insights into new market spaces rarely come from projecting the trend itself. Instead they arise from business insights into how the trend will change value to customers. By looking across time—from the value a market delivers today to the value it might deliver tomorrow—managers can actively shape their future and lay claim to new market space. Looking across time is perhaps more difficult than the previous approaches we've discussed, but it can be made subject to the same disciplined approach. We're not

Shifting the focus of strategy

From head-to-head competition to creating new market space

The conventional boundaries of competition	Head-to-head competition		Creating new market space
Industry	Focuses on rivals within its industry	→	Looks across substitute industries
Strategic group	Focuses on competitive position within strategic group	→	Looks across strategic groups within its industry
Buyer group	Focuses on better serving the buyer group	→	Redefines the buyer group of the industry
Scope of product and service offerings	Focuses on maximizing the value of product and service offerings within the bounds of its industry	→	Looks across to complementary product and service offerings that go beyond the bounds of its industry
Functional-emotional orientation of an industry	Focuses on improving price-performance in line with the functional-emotional orientation of its industry	→	Rethinks the functional-emotional orientation of its industry
Time	Focuses on adapting to external trends as they occur	→	Participates in shaping external trends over time

talking about predicting the future, which is inherently impossible. We're talking about finding insight in trends that are observable today. (See the diagram "Shifting the focus of strategy.")

Three principles are critical to assessing trends across time. To form the basis of a new value curve, these trends must be decisive to your business, they must be irreversible, and they must have a clear trajectory. Many trends can be observed at any one time—a discontinuity in technology, the rise of a new lifestyle, or a change in regulatory or social environments, for example. But usually only one or two will have a decisive impact on any particular business. And it may be possible to see a trend or major event without being able to predict its direction. In 1998, for example, the mounting Asian crisis was an important trend certain to have a big impact on financial services. But the direction that trend would take was impossible to predict— and therefore envisioning a new value curve that might result from it would have been a risky enterprise. In contrast, the euro is evolving along a constant trajectory as it replaces Europe's multiple currencies. This is a decisive, irreversible, and clearly developing trend upon which new market space might be created in financial services.

Having identified a trend of this nature, managers can then look across time and ask themselves what the market would look like if the trend were taken to its logical conclusion. Working back from that vision of a new value curve, they can then identify what must be changed today to unlock superior value for buyers.

Consider Enron, an energy company based in Houston, Texas. In the 1980s, Enron's business centered on gas pipelines. Deregulation of the gas industry was on the horizon. Such an event would certainly be decisive for Enron. The U.S. government had just deregulated the telecom and transportation industries, so a reversal in its intent to deregulate the gas industry was highly unlikely. Not only was the trend irreversible, its logical conclusion was also predictable—the end of price controls and the breakup of local gas monopolies. By assessing the gap between the market as it stood and the market as it was to be, Enron gained insight into how to create new market space.

When local gas monopolies were broken up, gas could be purchased from anywhere in the nation. At the time, the cost of gas varied dramatically from region to region. Gas was much more expensive, for example, in New York and Chicago than it was in Oregon and Idaho. Enron saw that deregulation would make possible a national market in which gas could be bought where it was cheap and sold where it was expensive. By examining how the gas market could operate with deregulation, Enron saw a way to unlock tremendous trapped value on a national scale.

Accordingly, Enron worked with government agencies to push for deregulation. It purchased regional gas-pipeline companies across the nation, tied them together, and created a national market for gas. That allowed Enron to buy the lowest cost gas from numerous sources across North America and to operate with the best spreads in the industry. Enron became the largest transporter of natural gas in North America, and its customers benefited from more reliable delivery and a drop in costs of as much as 40%.

Cisco Systems created a new market space in a similar way. It started with a decisive and irreversible trend that had a clear trajectory: the growing demand for high-speed data exchange. Cisco looked at the world as it was—and that world was hampered by slow data rates and incompatible computer networks. Demand was exploding as, among other factors, the number of Internet users doubled roughly every 100 days. So Cisco could clearly see that the problem would inevitably worsen. Cisco's routers, switches, and other networking devices were designed to create breakthrough value for customers, offering fast data exchanges in a seamless networking environment. Thus Cisco's insight is as much about value innovation as it is about technology. Today more than 80% of all traffic on the Internet flows through Cisco's products, and its margins in this new market space are in the 60% range.

Regenerating Large Companies

Creating new market space is critical not just for start-ups but also for the prosperity and survival of even the world's largest companies. Take Toyota as an example. Within three years of its launch in 1989, the Lexus accounted for nearly one-third of Toyota's operating profit while representing only 2% of its unit volume. Moreover, the Lexus boosted Toyota's brand image across its entire range of cars. Or think of Sony. The greatest contribution to Sony's profitable growth and its reputation in the last 20 years was the Walkman. Since its introduction in 1979, the Walkman has dominated the personal portable-stereo market, generating a huge positive spillover effect on Sony's other lines of business throughout the world.

Likewise, think of SMH. Its collection of watch companies ranges from Blancpain, whose watches retail for over $200,000, to Omega, the watch of astronauts, to midrange classics like Hamilton and Tissot to the sporty, chic watches of Longines and Rado. Yet it was the creation of the Swatch and the market of fun, fashionable watches that revitalized the entire Swiss watch industry and made SMH the darling of investors and customers the world over.

It is no wonder that corporate leaders throughout the world see market creation as a central strategic challenge to their organizations in the upcoming decade. They understand that in an overcrowded and demand-starved economy, profitable growth is not sustainable without creating, and re-creating, markets. That is what allows small companies to become big and what allows big companies to regenerate themselves.

Originally published in January 1999. Reprint 99105

Knowing a Winning Business Idea When You See One

IN 1998, MOTOROLA ROLLED OUT a product that was supposed to redefine the world of mobile telephony. The Iridium, declared the company, would be the first mobile phone to provide uninterrupted wireless communication anywhere in the world, no matter what the terrain or country. It was a complete flop. In its rush to embrace a new technology, Motorola overlooked the product's many drawbacks: the phone was heavy, it needed a host of attachments, and it couldn't be used in a car or building—exactly where jet-setting global executives needed it most. At $3,000, people couldn't see any compelling reason to switch from their $150 cell phones.

As this tale illustrates, even the most admired companies can get innovation spectacularly wrong. Sometimes companies rush a new technology to market too soon or at the wrong price. At other times, they ignore the radical idea that another company uses to put them out of business. CNN's competitors, for example, first dismissed its offerings as "Chicken Noodle News."

It's not as if companies don't know what the challenges of innovation are. A new product has to offer customers exceptional utility at an attractive price, and the company must be able to deliver it at a tidy profit. But the uncertainties surrounding innovation are so great that even the most insightful managers have a hard time evaluating the commercial readiness and potential of new business ideas.

Our Research on Innovation

MORE THAN A DECADE AGO, we researched the roots of profitable growth and found that innovation is the key driver—a finding consistent with the New Growth Theory of economics spearheaded by Paul Romer at Stanford University. Since then, our research has focused on how companies actually make innovations happen. We began by building up a comprehensive database that tracks over 30 successful, innovative companies in as many different industries.

Over time, as the Internet took off and dot-com companies began proliferating, our database expanded to include more than 100 companies—some that have succeeded at innovation and some that have failed. We have interviewed hundreds of managers at these companies and systematically compared their successes and failures.

In our previous HBR articles, we have drawn on our research to describe how the innovations of successful companies have reshaped their industries or even created new ones. (See "Value Innovation: The Strategic Logic of High Growth," and "Creating New Market Space," earlier in this volume.) We have also described how companies can create a working environment to generate, share, and build new ideas and knowledge. In this article, we move from the industries and companies to the innovations themselves. And we introduce a set of analytic tools that managers can use to assess the commercial potential of any innovative idea.

In this article, we offer a systematic approach to reducing the uncertainties of innovation. To understand what underpins the commercial success of a new idea, we've built up a database of more than 100 companies that have innovated successfully and repeatedly. We've also collected data on the companies whose products and services our innovators have displaced. (For more detail on our methodology, see the sidebar "Our Research on Innovation.") From that information, we created three analytic tools to help managers know a winning business idea when they see one—whatever the market space it occupies or creates. The first tool, "the buyer utility map," indicates the likelihood that customers will be attracted to the new idea. The second tool, "the price corridor of the mass," identifies what price will unlock the greatest number of customers. The third tool, "the business model guide," offers a framework for figuring out

Idea in Brief

Innovation's like a lottery, right? You have to pay for a lot of mistakes to hit the jackpot? Not necessarily. Though spotting winning business ideas can be challenging, Kim and Mauborgne recommend three tools that can remove much of the uncertainty:

- The **buyer utility map** helps you determine whether your idea would provide customers with unique forms of value that no one else offers.

- The **price corridor of the mass** tool enables you to estimate what price will attract the largest possible pool of buyers.

- The **business model guide** helps you figure out whether you can deliver the new offering to customers profitably.

These tools aren't the end of the story, though. To assure your idea's commercial viability, you'll also need to tackle stakeholders' resistance (such as employees worried that an innovation will threaten their livelihood).

whether and how a company can profitably deliver the new idea at the targeted price.

Applying the tools, though, is not the end of the story. Many innovations have had to overcome adoption hurdles—strong resistance from stakeholders both inside and outside the company. While often overlooked in the planning process, adoption hurdles can make or break the commercial viability of even the most powerful innovative ideas. So we'll conclude by discussing how managers can head off those reactions. First, though, let's look at utility.

Creating Exceptional Utility

The managers at Motorola responsible for the Iridium fell into a very common trap: they reveled in the bells and whistles of their new technology. But successful innovators focus on the product's utility—that is, they try to identify where and how the new product or service will change the lives of its consumers. Such a difference in perspective is important because it means that how a product is developed becomes less a function of its technical possibilities and more a function of its utility to customers.

Idea in Practice

Buyer Utility Map

How appealing will your interesting idea be to consumers? To answer this question, create a matrix. On the vertical axis, list forms of value (such as environmental friendliness, fun, or convenience). On the horizontal axis, list buyer-experience stages (e.g., purchase, delivery, use, supplements, maintenance, disposal). Plot the market's existing offerings on the matrix to show which forms of value they provide at which customer-experience stages.

Then determine how your new idea could stake out new spaces on the matrix.

Example: With its chic coffee bars and exotic mix of brews, Starbucks *offered a new form of value at the purchasing stage* by injecting fun and cachet into the coffee-buying experience.

Price Corridor of the Mass

What price for a potential innovation would capture the largest pool of customers To estimate this figure, first list alternative offerings to your idea. For instance, Southwest Airlines looked beyond other airlines' customers to people using buses, trains, and cars. Record the price and sales volume of each alternative. Analyze where the largest groups of existing customers are and what prices they currently pay.

Second, determine how high a price you can afford to set for these groups without opening the door

---

The buyer utility map helps to get managers thinking from the right perspective. It outlines all the levers companies can pull to deliver utility to customers as well as the different experiences customers can have of a product or service. This lets managers identify the full range of utility propositions that a product or service can offer. Let's look at the map's dimensions in detail. (See the exhibit "The buyer utility map.")

The six stages of the buyer experience cycle

A customer's experience can usually be broken down into a cycle of six distinct stages, running more or less sequentially from purchase to disposal. Each stage encompasses a wide variety of specific experiences. Purchasing, for example, includes the experience of browsing Amazon.com as well as the experience of pushing a shopping

for imitation products. If your innovation is protected legally through patents or copyrights, or if your company owns some exclusive asset (such as an established brand name), you can set a higher price.

Business Model Guide

Can you deliver the new innovation to the market profitably? This depends on your choices about materials, design, and manufacturing; business partnerships; and price models.

> *Example:* Swatch set a $40 price target for its watches. To make a profit at that price, it made smart choices about *materials, design, and manufacturing.* It used plastic (versus metal or leather), simplified the watches'

inner workings, and sealed its watchcases by ultrasonic welding instead of screws (a cheaper assembly technique).

> *Example:* ERP software leader SAP had serious gaps in its technology and distribution capabilities at its founding. To grow rapidly, it acquired these capabilities; for instance, by *partnering* with Oracle to gain access to the central database software sitting at the heart of SAP's core products R/2 and R/3.

> *Example:* Executive Jet's *price model*—buy the right to use a jet for a certain amount of time versus buying the jet itself—has made its aircraft accessible to a wide range of corporate customers.

cart through Wal-Mart's aisles. (The exhibit "Uncovering the buyer experience cycle" provides a set of questions that managers can ask to gauge the quality of the buyer's experience at each stage.)

The six utility levers

Cutting across the stages of the buyer's experience are what we call the levers of utility—the ways in which companies unlock utility for their customers. Most of the levers are obvious. Simplicity, fun and image, and environmental friendliness need little explanation. Nor does the idea that a product could reduce a customer's financial or physical risks. And a product or service offers convenience simply by being easy to obtain or use. The most commonly used lever—but perhaps the least obvious—is that of customer productivity. An innovation can increase customers' productivity by helping them

The buyer utility map

By locating a new product on one of the 36 spaces shown here, managers can clearly see how the new idea creates a different utility proposition from existing products.

The six stages of the buyer experience cycle

	Purchase	Delivery	Use	Supplements	Maintenance	Disposal
Customer productivity						
Simplicity						
Convenience						
Risk						
Fun and image						
Environmental friendliness						

The six utility levers

do their thing faster, better, or in different ways. The financial information company Bloomberg, for example, makes traders more efficient by offering on-line analytics that quickly analyze and compare the raw information it delivers.

By locating a new product on one of the 36 spaces of the buyer utility map, managers can clearly see how the new idea creates a different utility proposition from existing products. In our experience, managers all too often focus on delivering more of the same utility at the same stage of the buyer's experience. That approach may be reasonable in emerging industries, where there's plenty of room for

Uncovering the buyer experience cycle

A customer's product experience passes through six basic stages. To help companies assess the quality of a buyer's total experience, we have identified the key questions for each stage. Individually, these questions may be obvious, but taken together, they uncover the full picture of the experience cycle.

The buyer experience cycle

Purchase	Delivery	Use	Supplements	Maintenance	Disposal
How long does it take to find the product you need?	How long does it take to get the product delivered?	Does the product require training or expert assistance?	Do you need other products and services to make this product work?	Does the product require external maintenance?	Does use of the product create waste items?
Is the place of purchase attractive and accessible?	How difficult is it to unpack and install the new product?	Is the product easy to store when not in use?	If so, how costly are they?	How easy is it to maintain and upgrade the product?	How easy is it to dispose of the product?
How secure is the transaction environment?		How effective are the product's features and functions?			
How rapidly can you make a purchase?					

How Schwab created exceptional utility

ONE OF THE MOST INNOVATIVE companies in our database is the discount broker Charles Schwab. Schwab's first innovation was to make customers feel safe about trading over the phone and later online. At a time when most discount brokers were competing on price, Schwab recognized that customers were actually more concerned about the safe execution of their trades. By providing instantaneous computer confirmation, Schwab eliminated that perceived risk.

Schwab then went on to make purchasing more convenient. Most discount brokers were only open during normal office hours—which was not when customers were free. Customers' problems were compounded by the fact that they had to transfer the funds for their stock trades from their banks, which had even more restrictive hours and much slower response times than brokers. Schwab offered 24-hour, seven-day-a-week service and a Schwab One cash management account with checking privileges and Visa Card, allowing customers to sidestep those inconveniences.

Schwab's next innovation came in the simplicity and maintenance space. It saw how complex it was for customers to track their mutual fund investments. Customers would typically receive statements of their mutual fund accounts from each fund company they dealt with. They would then be burdened with putting all the pieces together to see the bigger picture of their financial performance. Schwab launched OneSource, a service that gives customers a monthly consolidated statement of all mutual fund investments purchased through Schwab. Schwab has gone on to explore new utility spaces and has kept ahead of the pack. Whether or not Schwab will continue

---

improving a company's current utility proposition. But in many existing industries, this approach is unlikely to produce market-shaping innovations. Let's look instead at how successful innovators have staked out new spaces on the map.

Using a new utility lever at the same stage. Many successful innovations create new expectations for a familiar experience. Starbucks, which has revolutionized the American office-worker's coffee break, is a case in point. Traditionally, people bought coffee in delis or fast-food chains—businesses that competed by offering customers fast and cheap coffee. In terms of the map, those companies focused on delivering customer productivity in the purchasing experience. Starbucks, however, moved into a new space entirely. By

to lead rests on its ability to keep staking out new utility spaces before its competitors do.

The six stages of the buyer experience cycle

		Purchase	Delivery	Use	Supplements	Maintenance	Disposal
The six utility levers	Customer productivity						
	Simplicity					OneSource	
	Convenience	24/7 service Schwab One cash management account					
	Risk	Secure transactions Instantaneous confirmations					
	Fun and image						
	Environmental friendliness						

establishing chic coffee bars that offer an exotic mix of brews, the company injected fun and cachet into the coffee-purchasing experience. As a result, middle class America has become coffee literate, and coffee bars have become American fixtures.

Using the same utility lever in a new stage. Companies can also innovate by extending a familiar utility to different parts of the customer's product or service experience. That's how Michael Dell changed the computer business. Computer manufacturers used to compete by offering faster computers with more features and software. In terms of the map, they offered customers more productivity in the use of the machines. Dell extended the same utility to the delivery experience. By bypassing dealers, Dell delivers

PCs tailored to customers' needs faster than any other computer manufacturer.

Using a new utility lever in a new stage. In some industries, the most rewarding innovations do something completely new. A good example of this kind of innovation is the Alto, a disposable fluorescent bulb manufactured by European electronics giant Philips. Most light bulb manufacturers competed to offer customers more productivity in use; they did not pay much attention to the fact that the bulbs had to be carted off to special dumping sites because of their harmful mercury content. By creating a fluorescent bulb that could be disposed of in an environmentally friendly manner, Philips moved into and dominated a utility space largely ignored by its competitors. In the first year alone, the Alto poached more than 25% of traditional fluorescent lamp sales in the United States while enjoying superior margins.

Beyond highlighting the differences between ideas that are genuine innovations and those that are essentially revisions of existing offerings, the buyer utility map reminds executives just how many unexplored innovation possibilities there are. Even the most productive innovators end up occupying only a small number of the 36 utility spaces. (For an example of how one innovative company's business ideas look on the map, see the sidebar "How Schwab Created Exceptional Utility.") Think for a moment of your own industry. How many spaces does your company occupy?

Setting a Strategic Price

Offering exceptional utility alone doesn't make an innovation successful. You also have to set the right price. In the old days, that wasn't such an immediate issue. Companies could test the waters by targeting novelty-seeking, price-insensitive customers at the launch and then drop prices over time to attract mainstream buyers. But in the new economy, managers have to know from the start what price will quickly create a large pool of customers.

There are two reasons why it has become critical to reach a high volume very quickly. First, companies are discovering that in more and more businesses, volume generates higher returns than it used to. That's because these days, as the nature of goods becomes more knowledge intensive, companies bear much more of their costs in product development than in manufacturing. So once the development costs have been covered, sales fall straight to the bottom line. A second reason is that some companies have no choice but to seize the mass market early. The value to a customer of a product or service such as the on-line auctions managed by eBay, for example, is closely tied to the total number of people using it. Customers who think hardly anyone else is using a product or service will not buy it either. As a result of this phenomenon, called network externalities, many products and services are an all-or-nothing proposition: either you sell millions at once or you sell nothing at all.

The price you choose for a product must not only attract customers in large numbers but also help you to retain them. We call this strategic pricing. Many innovations are extremely vulnerable to imitation. The Starbucks and Home Depot concepts, for example, are not ideas that can be protected by patents. For customers to remain loyal, they must be convinced that they will not find better value with an imitator. A company's reputation has to be earned on day one, because brand building these days relies heavily on word-of-mouth recommendations spreading rapidly through our networked society. Companies, therefore, must start with an offer that customers just can't refuse. Our next tool, the price corridor of the mass, will help managers find the right price for that irresistible offer—which, by the way, isn't necessarily the lowest price. The tool involves two distinct but interrelated steps. (See the exhibit "The price corridor of the mass.")

Step 1: Identifying the Price Corridor of the Mass

In setting a price, all companies look first at the products and services that most closely resemble their idea in terms of form—that is, other products within their industries. That's still a necessary exercise, of course, but market-shaping innovations win by creating new customer pools, not by just increasing the share of an existing

The price corridor of the mass

To find the right price for your new product, you must first identify the price corridor of the mass—that is, the price bandwidth that captures the largest groups of customers. Then, depending on how much legal and resource protection you have, determine how high a price you can set without inviting in competitors with imitation products.

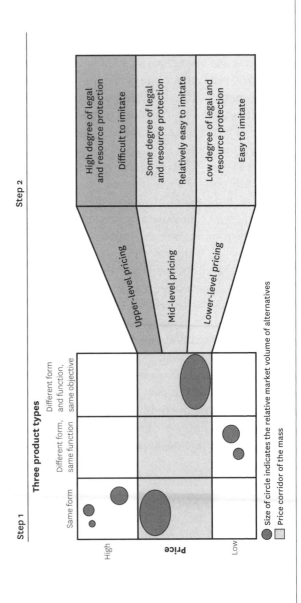

customer pool. So the main challenge in determining a strategic price is understanding the price sensitivities of people who will be comparing the new product with a host of very different-looking products and services offered by companies outside the group of traditional competitors. For some companies, identifying a product's potential customers is straightforward. In pricing short-haul trips, for example, Southwest Airlines only had to look beyond other airlines' customers to people using buses, trains, and cars. Other companies, however, may not find the exercise so easy. A good way to get executives to look outside their industry's boundaries is to have them list products and services that fall into two categories: those that take different forms but perform the same function, and those that take different forms and functions but share the same over-arching objective.

Different form, same function. Many successful innovations attract customers from other industries who use a product or service that performs the same function or core utility as the new one but takes a very different physical form. Most people who use Intuit's financial software package Quicken, for example, buy it not because it is a software product but because it helps them sort out their personal finances. The alternatives to using Quicken are to use pencil and paper—a tedious and error-prone approach—or to pay for the costly services of a CPA. The CPA, the pencil, and the software product offer the same functionality or core utility—namely, they help people organize and understand their financial affairs.

Different form and function, same objective. Some innovations have lured customers from even further away. The European cinema chain Kinepolis, for example, has diverted customers from a wide range of evening activities. In Brussels, it expanded the number of moviegoers by more than 40% with its first Megaplex. This growth came in part through drawing people away from other activities that differed in both form and function. For example, bars and restaurants have few physical features in common with a cinema. What's more, restaurants and bars serve a distinct function. They provide conversational and gastronomical pleasure—a very different experience from the visual entertainment that cinema offers. Yet despite these differences in form and function, people go to a bar or restaurant for the same broad reason they go to the movies—to enjoy a night out.

The exercise of listing the groups of alternative products and services will allow managers to see the full range of customers they can poach from other industries as well as from direct competitors. Managers should then graphically plot the price and volume of these alternatives, as shown in the exhibit. This provides a fairly straightforward way to identify where the largest groups of potential customers are and what prices they are prepared to pay for the products and services they currently use. The price bandwidth that captures the largest groups of customers is what we call the price corridor of the mass. In some cases, the range is very wide. For Southwest Airlines, for example, the largest groups of potential customers were paying on average $400 to buy an economy class short-haul ticket (short-haul being a 400-mile journey) or about $60 for the cost of going the same distance by car.

Step 2: Specifying a Level Within the Price Corridor

The second part of the tool helps managers determine how high a price they can afford to set within the corridor without inviting in competitors with imitation products. That assessment depends on the degree to which the product or service is protected legally through patents or copyrights and on the company's ownership of some exclusive asset, such as an expensive production plant or an established brand name. Obviously, companies that have no such protection must set a relatively low price. Going back to the Southwest Airlines example, because its service wasn't patentable and required no exclusive assets, its ticket prices fell in the lower boundary of the corridor—namely, against the price of car travel. But some products are protected enough to merit a high price. Dyson Vacuum Cleaners, for example, has been able to charge a high unit price for its bagless cleaners since the product's launch in 1995, thanks to both strong patents and an outstanding service capability. Few companies, however, are as insulated from competitors as Dyson is. Companies with uncertain patent and asset protection should consider pricing somewhere in the middle of the corridor.

Building a Profitable Business Model

Utility and price are only part of the story. At the end of the day, every company—dot-coms included—has to turn a profit. Successful innovators have lean and profitable business models from the outset. And a good business model is itself a powerful defense against imitation. The fact that CNN, for example, could produce 24 hours of news at one-fifth the hourly cost of network news fended off imitators for about 15 years.

There's no magic formula for finding that kind of business model, but we have developed a systematic way of thinking through the issues, which will help managers avoid some pitfalls. Our third tool, the business model guide, is a series of questions designed to open up the way managers think about production and distribution methods, their company's capabilities, and a pricing structure for the product. (See the exhibit "The business model guide.")

What is the cost target?

In our experience, companies have a hard time keeping down the costs of new products, and to compensate, they usually set prices far higher than would be strategically wise. Successful innovators, however, never let costs dictate price. By basing their cost targets on the market-driven strategic price and refusing to allow for overruns, they force their organizations to question virtually every assumption about materials, design, and manufacturing—often with surprising results.

The Swiss watch company Swatch is a case in point. At the start, founder Nicholas Hayek set a $40 price target for watches and mandated that the company create a product that could hit a target profit margin at that price. Given the high cost of Swiss labor, Swatch could achieve Hayek's goal only by making radical changes to the product and production methods. Instead of using the more traditional metal or leather, for example, Swatch used plastic. Swatch's

The business model guide

The questions "What is the cost target?" and "Who can we partner with?" are closely related. That's because a company's cost target will influence how it obtains the capabilities it needs, and the capabilities it needs will affect its ability to change its cost structure. Once costs and capabilities are optimized toward the cost target, which is driven by the strategic price, the company should challenge the industry's standard pricing model to reach more customers and increase profitability.

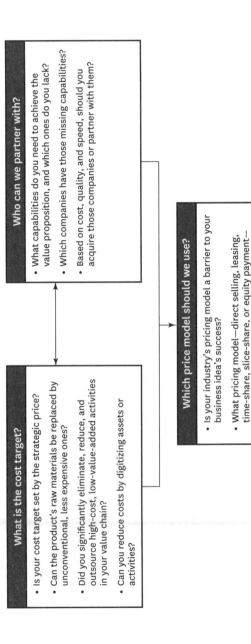

What is the cost target?

- Is your cost target set by the strategic price?
- Can the product's raw materials be replaced by unconventional, less expensive ones?
- Did you significantly eliminate, reduce, and outsource high-cost, low-value-added activities in your value chain?
- Can you reduce costs by digitizing assets or activities?

Who can we partner with?

- What capabilities do you need to achieve the value proposition, and which ones do you lack?
- Which companies have those missing capabilities?
- Based on cost, quality, and speed, should you acquire those companies or partner with them?

Which price model should we use?

- Is your industry's pricing model a barrier to your business idea's success?
- What pricing model—direct selling, leasing, time-share, slice-share, or equity payment— would create a greater profit pool?

engineers also drastically simplified the design of the watch's inner workings, reducing the number of parts from 150 to 51. Finally, the engineers developed new and cheaper assembly techniques—for instance, the watchcases were sealed by ultrasonic welding instead of screws. Taken together, the design and manufacturing changes enabled Swatch to reduce direct labor costs from 30% to less than 10% of total costs. In the end, the total manufacturing costs of the Swatch were almost 30% less than those of competing products from Hong Kong. These cost innovations let the Swiss company profitably compete in the mass market for watches—a market previously dominated by Asian manufacturers with a cheaper labor pool.

Who can we partner with?

In bringing a product to market, many innovators mistakenly try to carry out all the production and distribution activities themselves. Often, that's because they see the product as a platform for developing new capabilities. But unless the product is extremely well protected against imitation, this approach can be a recipe for disaster; time works against the innovator in favor of the imitator.

Consider EMI, which developed the CAT scanner, a medical device that earned creator Godfrey Houndsfield the Nobel Prize. Despite having no experience in the medical industry and no presence to speak of in the United States, the largest and most demanding market for advanced medical equipment, EMI tried to build its own distribution capability there. Unfortunately, the CAT scanner, although a medical breakthrough, was highly susceptible to imitation because its basic technologies were well established. Within three years, a host of CAT scanners manufactured by electronic giants like GE and Siemens were jostling for U.S. market share. The same year Houndsfield won his Nobel Prize, EMI had to sell its scanner unit to Thorn Electric.

Savvy innovators are increasingly eschewing organic growth and instead filling the gaps in their capabilities by partnering and acquiring. That allows them to move quickly and expertly. SAP, which rapidly grew to become the world leader in enterprise resource planning (ERP) software, had serious gaps both in its technology and in its distribution capabilities at its founding in 1972. Rather than cultivate capabilities internally, it acquired them. For example, SAP partnered with Oracle to gain access to the central database software that sits at the heart of SAP's core products R/2 and R/3. SAP also found partners to help it install and implement the product, namely consulting firms such as Arthur Andersen and Cap Gemini, which could leverage their strong networks among SAP's target customers. And it acquired companies such German-based iXOS Software to gain access to UNIX expertise rapidly. SAP's willingness to look outside the company to fill missing capabilities is one reason it has remained a world leader in business application software. And its success in the future will depend on its ability to keep reaching out in this way.

Which price model should we use?

Sometimes it seems that no amount of redesign or partnering will make it possible for a company to provide a product or service at the required strategic price. In such cases, it is very likely that managers have fallen into the trap of assuming too much about the way a product or service should be priced. When film videotapes first came out, for example, they were priced at around $80. Few people were willing to pay that amount because no one expected to watch the video more than two or three times.

Successful innovators never assume that there's only one way to price a product. Blockbuster Video, for example, got around the cost-price problem in its industry by changing the pricing model from selling to renting. At only a few dollars a rental, the home video market exploded; Blockbuster made more money by repeatedly renting the same $80 videos than it could have by selling them outright.

In addition to Blockbuster's rental model, innovators have used several other pricing models to bring expensive products within the reach of the mass market. One is the timeshare. The New Jersey company Executive Jet follows this model to make jets accessible to a wide range of corporate customers, who buy the right to use a jet for a certain amount of time rather than buying the jet itself. Another model is the slice-share; mutual fund managers, for instance, bring high-quality portfolio services—traditionally provided by private banks to the rich—to the small investor by selling a sliver of the portfolio rather than its whole. Some companies are abandoning the concept of price altogether. Instead, they give products to customers in return for an equity interest in the customer's business. Hewlett-Packard, for example, trades high-powered servers to Silicon Valley start-ups for a share of their revenues. The customers get immediate access to a key capability, and HP stands to earn a lot more than the price of the machine. The aim is not to compromise on the strategic price but to hit the target through a new price model.

Overcoming Adoption Hurdles

Even an outstanding value proposition and an unbeatable business model may not be enough to guarantee a product's success. Almost by definition, innovations threaten the status quo, and for that reason often provoke fear and resistance among a company's three main stakeholders—its employees, its business partners, and the general public. Would-be innovators ignore those reactions at their peril. As with most fears, the way to overcome a fear of innovation is by educating the fearful.

Employees

Failure to adequately address the concerns of employees about the impact an innovation may have on their livelihoods can be expensive. When Merrill Lynch's management, for example, announced plans to create an on-line brokerage service, its stock price fell by 14% as reports emerged of resistance and infighting within the company's large retail brokerage division. Smart innovators, therefore, make a concerted effort to communicate to employees that the company is aware of the threats an innovation poses before going public with it. They work with employees to find ways of defusing the threats so that everyone in the company wins, despite shifts in people's roles, responsibilities, and rewards. In contrast to Merrill Lynch, Morgan Stanley Dean Witter engaged employees in an open internal discussion of the company's strategy for meeting the challenge of the Internet. Morgan's efforts paid off handsomely. Because the market realized that Morgan's employees understood the need for an e-venture, the company's shares rose by 13% when it eventually announced the venture.

Business partners
Potentially even more damaging than employee disaffection is the resistance of partners who fear that their revenue streams or market positions are threatened by a new idea. That was the problem faced by SAP when it was developing its product AcceleratedSAP (ASAP)—a faster-to-implement version of R/3. ASAP brought ERP within the reach of midsized and small companies for the first time. The problem was that the development of best-practice templates for ASAP required the active cooperation of large consulting firms that were deriving substantial income from implementations of SAP's other products. SAP resolved the dilemma by openly discussing the issues with its partners. Its executives convinced the consulting firms that they stood to gain more business by cooperating. Although ASAP would reduce implementation time for small and midsized companies, consultants would gain access to a new ERP client base that would more than compensate for some lost revenues from larger companies. It would also offer consultants a way to respond to customers' increasingly vocal concerns that ERP software took too long to implement.

The general public
Opposition to an innovation can also spread to the general public—especially if the innovation is the result of a technological breakthrough that threatens established social or political norms. The effects can be devastating. Consider Monsanto, which makes genetically modified foods. It has become a figure of questionable intentions among European consumers—who should be customers—thanks to the efforts of environmental groups such as Greenpeace, Friends of the Earth, and the Soil Association. The attacks of these groups have struck many chords in Europe, which

has a history of environmental concern and powerful agricultural lobbies.

Monsanto's mistake was to let other people take charge of the debate. It should have educated both the environmental groups and the public on the benefits of genetically modified food and its potential to eliminate world famine and disease. Once the products came out, Monsanto should have given consumers a choice between organic and genetically modified foods by labeling which products had genetically modified seeds as their base. Had Monsanto taken these steps, instead of being vilified, it might have ended up as the "Intel Inside" of food for the future—the provider of the essential technology.

In educating these three groups of stakeholders, the key challenge is to engage in an open discussion about why the innovation is necessary, explain its merits, and set clear expectations of the innovation's ramifications and how the company will address them. Stakeholders need to know that their voices have been heard and that there will be no surprises. Companies that take the trouble to have such a dialogue with stakeholders will find that it amply repays the time and effort involved. (For a fuller discussion of how companies can engage stakeholders—employees in particular—see our article "Fair Process: Managing in the Knowledge Economy" earlier in this volume.

Troubles like Motorola's Iridium and Monsanto's genetically modified foods give innovation a bad name. But when innovations do succeed they can create compelling new businesses and even whole new industries. AOL, for instance, did more than create an Internet portal; it virtually created the industry of Internet service providers. With all the uncertainties around innovation, it is perhaps unsurprising that many managers regard it as something of a lottery: you have to pay for a lot of mistakes to hit the jackpot. There's some truth in that view, of course. There will always be an element of chance—even magic—about innovation. No one has a crystal ball.

But we believe that the framework presented here strips much of the mystery away and brings innovation firmly into the realm of plannable business. If a new idea passes its evaluation by the tools introduced here, and if it is fairly communicated to stakeholders, managers can be confident that they have found a winner. But our framework does more than just evaluate individual new ideas. By revealing what makes a new idea a commercial success, it enables companies to develop a coherent strategy for becoming successful at business innovation. To put it another way, the tools help companies not only to recognize a winner when they see one but also to know where to start looking in the first place.

Originally published in September–October 2000. Reprint R00510

Charting Your Company's Future

JOHN REED OF CITICORP was known for insisting that his executives get the big picture. As chairman and CEO, he demanded that business unit heads present their proposed strategies in no more than a few slides. Executives who failed to meet Reed's exacting standards for brevity met with his unconcealed displeasure. And if it happened too often, they ran the risk of being left out of the loop on future strategy sessions.

Many leaders share Reed's obsession with the big picture, yet our research shows that few companies actually have a clear strategic vision. The problem, we believe, stems from the strategic-planning process itself. The process usually involves the preparation of a large document—culled from a mishmash of data provided by people from various parts of the organization who often have conflicting agendas and poor communication. The report typically begins with a lengthy description of the industry and the competitive situation. There follows a discussion of how to increase market share here and there, capture new segments, or cut costs, which leads to an outline of numerous goals and initiatives. A full budget is almost invariably attached, as are lavish graphs and a surfeit of spreadsheets.

No wonder so few strategic plans turn into action; executives are paralyzed by the muddle. But it doesn't have to be that way. We suggest an alternative approach to strategic planning, based not on preparing a document but on drawing a picture we call a "strategy canvas." This approach consistently produces strategies that are easy to understand and communicate, that engage more people within an organization, and that unlock the creativity of participants. In the following pages, we'll describe how one leading European financial services company used our approach, to notable effect. First, though, let's look at what makes a good strategy canvas.

Revealing Your Strategic Profile

Academics and consultants have developed an armory of tools to help companies understand their strategic positioning, and many of those tools have yielded successful strategies. Our approach—drawing a strategy canvas—is unique because it does three things in one picture. First, it shows the strategic profile of an industry by depicting very clearly the factors that affect competition among industry players, as well as those that might in the future. Second, it shows the strategic profile of current and potential competitors, identifying which factors they invest in strategically. Finally, our approach draws the company's strategic profile—or value curve—showing how it invests in the factors of competition and how it might invest in them in the future. The basic component of our strategy canvas, the value curve, is a tool we developed in our research and consulting work. (For a full description, see "Value Innovation: The Strategic Logic of High Growth" and "Creating New Market Space," earlier in this volume.)

To illustrate how a strategy canvas works, we'll take you through one we've created for the short-haul airline industry. In the exhibit "The strategy canvas of the short-haul airline industry," the factors of competition for the industry are listed on the horizontal axis. The vertical axis indicates the degree to which airlines and the providers of alternative services invest in the competitive factors. A relatively low position means a company invests less and, hence, offers less in that factor—or, in the case of price, asks for less. If you look at meals, for example, Southwest provides little in the way of free refreshment, though not as little as you would get if you drove yourself. By connecting the dots across all the factors for each player, you reveal the strategic profiles of Southwest, its direct competitors, and its main alternative, the car.

The strategy canvas of the short-haul airline industry

The strategic profile of Southwest Airlines differs dramatically from those of its competitors in the short-haul airline industry. Note how Southwest's profile has more in common with the car's than with the profile of other airlines.

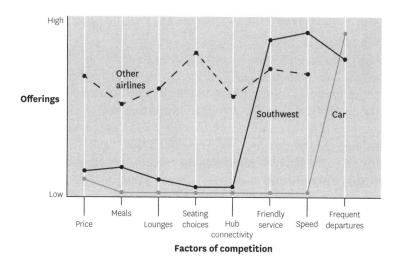

Southwest Airline's profile is a perfect example of a good strategy, because it shows the three complementary qualities that characterize an effective strategy: focus, divergence, and a compelling tag line. If your company's strategic profile does not clearly reveal those qualities, your strategy will likely be muddled, undifferentiated, and hard to communicate.

Focus

Every great strategy has focus, and a company's strategic profile, or value curve, should clearly show it. Looking at Southwest's profile, for example, you can see at once that the company emphasizes just three factors: friendly service, speed, and frequent point-to-point departures. By focusing in this way, Southwest has been able to price against car transportation; it doesn't make extra investments in meals, lounges, and seating choices. By contrast, Southwest's traditional competitors invest in all the airline industry's competitive factors, which makes it much more difficult for them to match Southwest's prices. Across-the-board investing is often a sign that competitors' moves are setting a company's agenda.

Divergence

When a company's strategy is formed reactively as it tries to keep up with the competition, it loses its uniqueness. Consider the similarities in most airlines' meals and business-class lounges. On the strategy canvas, therefore, reactive strategists tend to share a profile. Indeed, in the case of Southwest, we found that the value curves of the company's competitors were virtually identical, which is why they share the same value curve in the exhibit. By contrast, the value curves of innovators' strategies always stand apart. They might eliminate or substantially reduce investments in certain factors, or they might dramatically increase investments in others. Sometimes they even create new factors, thereby changing the industry's overall profile. Southwest, for instance, pioneered point-to-point travel between midsize cities; previously, the industry operated through hub-and-spoke systems.

Compelling tag line

The final test of a good strategy picture is how well it lends itself to a tag line. "The speed of the plane at the price of the car—whenever you need it." That's the tag line of Southwest Airlines, or at least it could be. What could Southwest's competitors say? Even the most proficient ad agency would have difficulty reducing the conventional offering of lunches, seat choices, lounges, and hub links with standard service, slower speeds, and higher prices into a memorable tag line. A good tag line must not only deliver a clear message but also advertise an offering truthfully, or else customers will lose trust and interest. If you can't come up with a strong and authentic tag line, chances are you don't have a strong strategy, either.

Drawing Your Strategy Canvas

Drawing a strategy canvas is never easy. Even identifying the key factors of competition is far from straightforward. As we shall see, the final list is usually very different from the first draft.

Assessing to what extent your company and its competitors offer the various factors is equally challenging. Most managers have a strong impression of how they and their competitors fare along one or two dimensions within their own scope of responsibility, but very few are able to see the overall dynamics of their industry. The catering manager of an airline, for instance, will be highly sensitive to how his airline compares in terms of refreshments. But that focus makes consistent measurement difficult; what seems to be a very big difference to the catering manager may not be so important to customers, who look at the complete offering. Some managers will define the competitive factors according to internal benefits. For example, a CIO might prize his company's IT infrastructure for its data-mining capacity, a feature lost on most customers, who are more concerned with speed and ease of use.

Over the years, we've developed a structured process for drawing and discussing a strategy canvas that results in the creation of distinct and communicable strategies. It was recently adopted by a 150-year-old financial services group that we'll call European Financial Services (EFS). Through the process, EFS developed a strategy that has boosted overall revenues by 30%. The process, which involves a lot of visual stimulation in order to unlock people's creativity, has four major steps.

Visual awakening

A common mistake people make is to discuss changes to strategy before resolving differences of opinion about the current state of play. Another problem is that executives are often slow to accept the need for change; they may have a vested interest in the status quo, or they may feel that time will eventually vindicate their previous choices. Indeed, when we ask executives what prompts them to introduce change, they usually say that it takes a very determined leader or a real crisis.

The strategy canvas of corporate foreign exchange

When EFS executives compared the strategic profiles of the main players in the traditional corporate foreign exchange business, they discovered some alarming similarities. In fact, EFS and its nonbank competitors actually shared the same profile. The profile of commercial banks, the other providers of corporate foreign exchange services, also resembled the EFS profile in many respects.

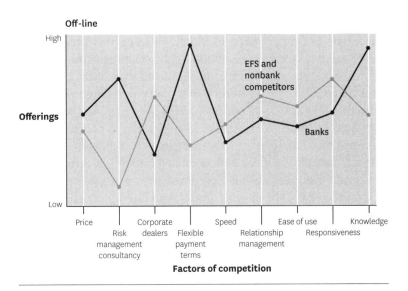

Fortunately, we've found that asking executives to draw the value curve of their company's strategy brings forcefully home the need for change. It serves as a wake-up call. That was certainly the experience at EFS, which had been struggling for a long time with an ill-defined and poorly communicated strategy. The company was also deeply divided: The top executives of EFS's regional subsidiaries bitterly resented what they saw as the arrogance of the corporate executives. That conflict made it all the more difficult for EFS to come to grips with its strategic problems; before executives can chart a new strategy, they must reach a common understanding of the company's current position.

In this strategy canvas, EFS executives compared their company's on-line strategy with that of Clearskies and other competitors. Note how focused and unique Clearskies' profile is, while EFS's is virtually identical to that of the other on-line foreign exchange service providers.

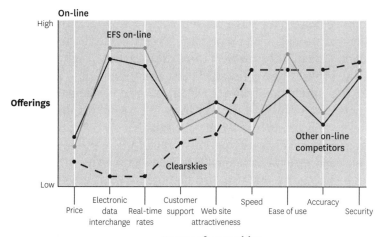

Factors of competition

EFS began the strategy process by bringing together more than 20 senior managers from subsidiaries in Europe, North America, Asia, and Australia and splitting them into two teams. One team was responsible for producing a value curve depicting EFS's current strategic profile in its traditional corporate foreign exchange business relative to its competitors. The other team was charged with the same task for EFS's emerging on-line foreign exchange business. They were given just 90 minutes because if EFS had a clear strategy, it would surely emerge quickly.

It turned out to be a painful experience. Both teams had heated debates about what constituted a competitive factor and what the factors were. Different factors were important, it seemed, in different regions and even for different customer segments. For example, Europeans argued that in its traditional business, EFS had to offer consulting services on risk management, given the perceived risk-averse nature of its customers. Americans, however, dismissed that as largely irrelevant; they stressed the value of speed and ease of use. Many people had pet ideas of which they were the sole champions. One person in the on-line team argued, for instance, that customers would be drawn in by the promise of instant confirmations of their transactions—a service no one else thought necessary. Despite these difficulties, the teams completed their assignments and presented their pictures in a general meeting of all participants. Their results are shown in the exhibit "The strategy canvas of corporate foreign exchange."

The pictures clearly revealed defects in the company's strategy. EFS's traditional and on-line value curves both demonstrated a serious lack of focus; the company was investing in diverse and numerous factors in both businesses. What's more, EFS's two curves were very similar to competitors'. Unsurprisingly, neither team could come up with a memorable tag line that was true to the team's value curve. The pictures also highlighted contradictions: The on-line business, for example, had invested heavily in making the Web site easy to use—it had even won awards for this—but it became apparent that speed of use had been overlooked. EFS had one of the slowest Web sites in the business, which might explain why such a well-regarded site did a relatively poor job of attracting customers. The sharpest shocks, perhaps, came from comparing EFS's strategy with its competitors'. The on-line group realized that its strongest competitor, which we've called Clearskies, had a focused, original, and easily communicable strategy: "One click E-Z FX."

Faced with direct evidence of the company's shortcomings, EFS's executives could not defend what they had shown to be a weak, unoriginal, and poorly communicated strategy. Trying to draw the strategy canvases had made a stronger case for change than any argument based on numbers and words could have done.

Visual exploration

Getting the wake-up call is just the first step; a strategy still must be conceived. So the next step is to send a team into the field, putting managers face-to-face with what they have to make sense of: how people use their products. This may seem obvious, yet we have

The Four Steps of Visualizing Strategy

Visual Awakening

- Compare your business with your competitors' by drawing your "as is" strategy picture.
- See where your strategy needs to change.

Visual Exploration

Go into the field to:

- discover the adoption hurdles for noncustomers.
- observe the distinctive advantages of alternative products and services.
- see which factors you should eliminate, create, or change.

Visual Strategy Fair

- Draw your "to be" strategy canvases based on insights from field observations.
- Get feedback on alternative strategy pictures from customers, lost customers, competitors' customers, and noncustomers.
- Use feedback to build the best "to be" strategy.

Visual Communication

- Distribute your before-and-after strategic profiles on one page for easy comparison.
- Support only those projects and operational moves that allow your company to close the gaps to actualize the new strategy.

found that managers all too often outsource this part of the strategy-making process. They rely on reports that other people (often at one or two removes from the world they report on) have put together.

There is simply no substitute for seeing for yourself. Great artists don't paint from other people's descriptions or even from photographs—they like to see the subject for themselves. The same is true for great strategists. Michael Bloomberg, New York City's mayor, was hailed as a business genius for his realization that the providers of financial information needed also to provide on-line analytics to help users make sense of the data. But he would be the first to tell you that the idea should have been obvious to anybody who had ever *watched* traders using Reuters or Dow Jones Telerate. Before Bloomberg, traders used paper, pencil, and handheld calculators to take down price quotes and figure fair market values before making buy and sell decisions, which cost them both time and money and built in errors. Great strategic insights like this are less the product of genius than of getting into the field.

Obviously, the first port of call should be the customers. But you should not stop there. You should also go after lost customers, competitors' customers, and, where relevant, the customers' customers. And when the customer is not the same as the user, you need to extend your observations to the users, as Bloomberg did. You should not only talk to these people but also watch them in action. Identifying the array of complementary products and services that are consumed alongside your own may give you insight into bundling opportunities. For example, couples who go to the movies will engage a babysitter for the night. Adding on-site child care services helped the Bert Claeys Group, owners of the cinema chain Kinepolis, fill theaters in Europe. Finally, you need to look at how customers might find alternative ways of fulfilling the need that your product serves. For instance, driving is an alternative to flying, so its distinct advantages and characteristics should also be examined.

EFS sent its managers into the field for four weeks. Each was to interview and observe ten people involved in corporate foreign exchange, including lost customers, new customers, and the customers of EFS's competitors. The managers also reached outside the industry's traditional boundaries to companies that did not yet use corporate foreign exchange services but that might in the future, such as Internet-based companies with a global reach like Amazon.com. They interviewed the end users of corporate foreign exchange services—the accounting and treasury departments of companies. And finally, they looked at ancillary products and services that their customers used—in particular, treasury management and pricing simulations.

The field research overturned many of the conclusions managers had reached in the first step of the strategy creation process. For instance, account relationship managers, which nearly everyone had agreed were a key to success, and on which EFS prided itself, turned out to be the company's Achilles' heel. Customers hated wasting time dealing with relationship managers.

To everyone's astonishment, the factor customers valued most was getting speedy confirmation of transactions, which only one manager had previously suggested was important. EFS's managers saw that their customers' accounting-department personnel spent a lot of time making phone calls to confirm that payments had been made and to check when they would be received. Numerous calls were also received on the same subject, and the time wasted in handling them was compounded by the necessity of making further calls to the foreign exchange provider, namely EFS or a competitor.

EFS's teams were then sent back to the drawing board. This time, though, they had to propose a new strategy. Each team had to draw six new and different value curves, each one depicting a strategy that would make the company stand out in its market. By demanding six pictures from each team, we hoped to push managers to create innovative proposals. For each visual strategy, the teams also had to write a compelling tag line that captured the essence of the strategy and spoke directly to buyers. Suggestions included "Leave It to Us," "Make Me Smarter," and "Transactions in Trust."

Visual strategy fair

After two weeks of drawing and redrawing, the teams presented their strategy canvases at what we call a "visual strategy fair." Attendees included senior corporate executives but consisted mainly of representatives of EFS's external constituencies, the kinds of people the managers had met with during their field trips. In just two hours, the teams presented all 12 curves, figuring that any idea that takes more than ten minutes to communicate is probably too complicated to be any good. The pictures were hung on the walls so that the audience could easily see them.

After the 12 strategies were presented, the judges–the invited attendees–were each given five Post-it Notes and told to put one next to their favorites. They could put all five on a single strategy if they found it that compelling. The transparency and immediacy of this approach freed it from the politics that sometimes seem endemic to the strategic-planning process. Managers had to rely on the originality and clarity of their curves and their pitches. One began, for instance, with the line "We've got a strategy so cunning that you won't be our customers, you'll be our fans."

After the notes were posted, the judges were asked to explain their picks, adding another level of feedback to the strategy-making process. Judges were also asked to explain why they did not vote for value curves.

As the teams synthesized the judges' common likes and dislikes, they realized that fully one-third of what they had thought were key competitive factors were, in fact, marginal to customers. Another third either were not well articulated or had been overlooked in the visual-awakening phase. It was clear that they needed to reassess some long-held assumptions, such as EFS's separation of its on-line and traditional businesses. They also learned that buyers from all markets had a basic set of needs and expected similar services. If you met those particular needs, customers would happily forgo everything else. Regional differences became significant only when there was a problem with the basics. This was news to many people who had claimed that their regions were unique.

Following the strategy fair, the teams were finally able to complete their mission. They could draw a value curve that was a truer likeness of the existing strategic profile than anything they had produced earlier, partly because the new picture ignored the specious distinction that EFS had made between its on-line and off-line businesses. More important, they were now in a position to draw a new curve that would both be distinctive and speak to a true but hidden need in the marketplace. See the exhibit "EFS: Before and after."

As the graphic shows, the new strategy completely eliminated relationship management and reduced investment in account executives, who, from this point on, were assigned only to "AAA" accounts. EFS's new strategy emphasized ease of use, security, accuracy, and speed. These factors would be delivered through computerization,

EFS: Before and after

This picture was the final result of EFS's strategy creation process. Since then, investment decisions have been made on the basis of how they will enable the company to shift from the old curve to the new one. The "before" curve has been revised to combine the on-line and off-line businesses, and a number of nonessential factors were removed from consideration in the process. The "after" strategy changes the industry's overall strategic profile by eliminating relationship management and adding confirmation and tracking services.

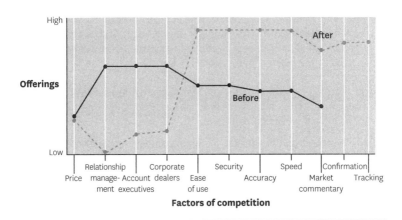

which would allow customers to input data directly instead of having to send a fax to EFS. This action would also free up corporate dealers' time, a large portion of which had been spent completing paperwork and correcting errors. Even though their numbers were reduced, corporate dealers would now be able to provide richer market commentary, a key success factor. Using the Internet, EFS would send automatic confirmations to all customers. And it would offer a payment-tracking service, just as FedEx and UPS do for parcels. The foreign exchange industry had never offered these services before.

The new value curve exhibited the criteria of a successful strategy. It displayed more focus than the previous strategy—investments that were made were given a much stronger commitment than

Using Strategy Canvases at the Corporate Level

VISUALIZING STRATEGY CAN GREATLY INFORM the dialogue among individual business units and the corporate center. When business units present their strategy canvases to one another, they deepen their understanding of the other businesses in the corporate portfolio. Moreover, the process also fosters the transfer of strategic-planning best practices across units.

To see how this works, consider how Samsung Electronics of Korea used strategy canvases at its corporate conference in 2000, which was attended by more than 70 top managers, including the CEO. Unit heads presented their canvases and implementation plans to senior executives and to one another. Discussions were heated, and a number of unit heads argued that the freedom of their units to form new strategies was constrained by the degree of competition they faced; poor performers felt they had little option but to match their competitors' offerings. That hypothesis was proven false when one of the fastest-growing units—the mobile phone business—presented its strategy canvas. Not only did the unit have a distinctive value curve, it also faced the most intense competition.

Do your business unit heads lack an understanding of the other businesses in your corporate portfolio? Are your strategic-planning best practices poorly communicated across your business units? Are your low-performing units quick to blame their competitive situations for their results? If you answered yes to any of these questions, try drawing, and then sharing, the strategy canvases of your business units.

---

before. It also stood apart from the industry's existing me-too curves and lent itself to a compelling tag line: "The Federal Express of corporate foreign exchange: easy, reliable, fast, and trackable."

Visual communication

Once the new strategy is set, the last step is communicating it in a way that can be easily understood by any employee. EFS distributed the one-page picture showing its new and old strategic profiles so that every employee could see where the company stood and where they had to focus their efforts. The senior managers who participated in developing the strategy held meetings with their direct reports to walk them through the picture, explaining what needed to be eliminated, reduced, raised, and created to achieve the new strategy. Those people passed the message on to their direct reports. Employees were so motivated by the clear game plan that many pinned up a version of the picture in their cubicles as a reminder of EFS's new priorities and the gaps that needed to be closed.

The new picture became a reference point for all investment decisions. Only those ideas that would help EFS move from the old to the new value curve were given the go-ahead. When, for example, regional offices requested the IT department to add links on the Web site, which in the past would have been agreed to without debate, IT asked them to explain how the new links helped move EFS toward its new profile. If the regional offices couldn't provide an explanation, the request was denied. Likewise, when the IT department pitched a multimillion-dollar back-office system to top management, the system's ability to meet the new value curve's strategic needs was the chief metric by which it was judged.

———————

Drawing a strategy canvas is not, of course, the only part of the strategic-planning process. At some stage, numbers and documents must be compiled and discussed. But we believe that the details will fall into place more easily if managers start with the big picture. Completing the four steps of visualizing strategy will put strategy back into strategic planning, and it will greatly improve your chances of coming up with a winning formula. As Aristotle pointed out: "The soul never thinks without an image."

Originally published in June 2002. Reprint R0206D

Tipping Point
Leadership

IN FEBRUARY 1994, William Bratton was appointed police commissioner of New York City. The odds were against him. The New York Police Department, with a $2 billion budget and a workforce of 35,000 police officers, was notoriously difficult to manage. Turf wars over jurisdiction and funding were rife. Officers were underpaid relative to their counterparts in neighboring communities, and promotion seemed to bear little relationship to performance. Crime had gotten so far out of control that the press referred to the Big Apple as the Rotten Apple. Indeed, many social scientists had concluded, after three decades of increases, that New York City crime was impervious to police intervention. The best the police could do was react to crimes once they were committed.

Yet in less than two years, and without an increase in his budget, Bill Bratton turned New York into the safest large city in the nation. Between 1994 and 1996, felony crime fell 39%; murders, 50%; and theft, 35%. Gallup polls reported that public confidence in the NYPD jumped from 37% to 73%, even as internal surveys showed job satisfaction in the police department reaching an all-time high. Not surprisingly, Bratton's popularity soared, and in 1996, he was featured on the cover of *Time*. Perhaps most impressive, the changes have outlasted their instigator, implying a fundamental shift in the department's organizational culture and strategy. Crime rates have continued to fall: Statistics released in December 2002 revealed that New York's overall crime rate is the lowest among the 25 largest cities in the United States.

The NYPD turnaround would be impressive enough for any police chief. For Bratton, though, it is only the latest of no fewer than five successful turnarounds in a 20-year career in policing. In the hope that Bratton can repeat his New York and Boston successes, Los Angeles has recruited him to take on the challenge of turning around the LAPD. (For a summary of his achievements, see the table "Bratton in action.")

So what makes Bill Bratton tick? As management researchers, we have long been fascinated by what triggers high performance or suddenly brings an ailing organization back to life. In an effort to find the common elements underlying such leaps in performance, we have built a database of more than 125 business and nonbusiness organizations. Bratton first caught our attention in the early 1990s, when we heard about his turnaround of the New York Transit Police. Bratton was special for us because in all of his turnarounds, he succeeded in record time despite facing all four of the hurdles that managers consistently claim block high performance: an organization wedded to the status quo, limited resources, a demotivated staff, and opposition from powerful vested interests. If Bratton could succeed against these odds, other leaders, we reasoned, could learn a lot from him.

Over the years, through our professional and personal networks and the rich public information available on the police sector, we have systematically compared the strategic, managerial, and performance records of Bratton's turnarounds. We have followed up by interviewing the key players, including Bratton himself, as well as many other people who for professional—or sometimes personal— reasons tracked the events.

Our research led us to conclude that all of Bratton's turnarounds are textbook examples of what we call tipping point leadership. The theory of tipping points, which has its roots in epidemiology, is well known; it hinges on the insight that in any organization, once the beliefs and energies of a critical mass of people are engaged, conversion to a new idea will spread like an epidemic, bringing about fundamental change very quickly. The theory suggests that such a movement can be unleashed only by agents who make unforgettable

Idea in Brief

How can you overcome the hurdles facing any organization struggling to change: addiction to the status quo, limited resources, demotivated employees, and opposition from powerful vested interests?

Take lessons from police chief Bill Bratton, who's pulled the trick off five times. Most dramatically, he transformed the U.S.'s most dangerous city—New York—into

its safest. Bratton used **tipping point leadership** to make unarguable calls for change, concentrate resources on what really mattered, mobilize key players' commitment, and silence naysayers.

Not every executive has Bratton's personality, but most have his potential—if they follow his success formula.

and unarguable calls for change, who concentrate their resources on what really matters, who mobilize the commitment of the organization's key players, and who succeed in silencing the most vocal naysayers. Bratton did all of these things in all of his turnarounds.

Most managers only dream of pulling off the kind of performance leaps Bratton delivered. Even Jack Welch needed some ten years and tens of millions of dollars of restructuring and training to turn GE into the powerhouse it is today. Few CEOs have the time and money that Welch had, and most—even those attempting relatively mild change—are soon daunted by the scale of the hurdles they face. Yet we have found that the dream can indeed become a reality. For what makes Bratton's turnarounds especially exciting to us is that his approach to overcoming the hurdles standing in the way of high performance has been remarkably consistent. His successes, therefore, are not just a matter of personality but also of method, which suggests that they can be replicated. Tipping point leadership is learnable.

In the following pages, we'll lay out the approach that has enabled Bratton to overcome the forces of inertia and reach the tipping point. We'll show first how Bratton overcame the cognitive hurdles that block companies from recognizing the need for radical change. Then we'll describe how he successfully managed around the public sector's endemic constraints on resources, which he even turned to his advantage. In the third section, we'll explain how Bratton overcame

Idea in Practice

Four Steps to the Tipping Point

1. Break through the cognitive hurdle.

To make a compelling case for change, don't just point at the numbers and demand better ones. Your abstract message won't stick. Instead, make key managers *experience* your organization's problems.

> *Example:* New Yorkers once viewed subways as the most dangerous places in their city. But the New York Transit Police's senior staff pooh-poohed public fears—because none had ever ridden subways. To shatter their complacency, Bratton required all NYTP officers—himself included—to commute by subway. Seeing the jammed turnstiles, youth gangs, and derelicts, they grasped the need for change—and embraced responsibility for it.

2. Sidestep the resource hurdle.

Rather than trimming your ambitions (dooming your company to mediocrity) or fighting for more resources (draining attention from the underlying problems), concentrate *current* resources on areas *most* needing change.

> *Example:* Since the majority of subway crimes occurred at only a few stations, Bratton focused manpower there—instead of putting a cop on every subway line, entrance, and exit.

3. Jump the motivational hurdle.

To turn a mere strategy into a movement, people must recognize what needs to be done and yearn to do it themselves. But don't try reforming your whole organization; that's cumbersome and expensive. Instead, motivate *key influencers*—persuasive

---

the motivational hurdles that had discouraged and demoralized even the most eager police officers. Finally, we'll describe how Bratton neatly closed off potentially fatal resistance from vocal and powerful opponents. (For a graphic summary of the ideas expressed in this article, see the figure "Tipping point leadership at a glance.")

Break Through the Cognitive Hurdle

In many turnarounds, the hardest battle is simply getting people to agree on the causes of current problems and the need for change.

people with multiple connections. Like bowling kingpins hit straight on, they topple all the other pins. Most organizations have several key influencers who share common problems and concerns—making it easy to identify and motivate them.

Example: Bratton put the NYPD's key influencers—precinct commanders—under a spotlight during semiweekly crime strategy review meetings, where peers and superiors grilled commanders about precinct performance. Results? A culture of performance, accountability, and learning that commanders replicated down the ranks.

Also make challenges attainable. Bratton exhorted staff to make NYC's streets safe "block by block, precinct by precinct, and borough by borough."

4. Knock over the political hurdle.

Even when organizations reach their tipping points, powerful vested interests resist change. Identify and silence key naysayers early by putting a respected senior insider on your top team.

Example: At the NYPD, Bratton appointed 20-year veteran cop John Timoney as his number two. Timoney knew the key players and how they played the political game. Early on, he identified likely saboteurs and resisters among top staff—prompting a changing of the guard.

Also, silence opposition with indisputable facts. When Bratton proved his proposed crime-reporting system required less than 18 minutes a day, time-crunched precinct commanders adopted it.

Most CEOs try to make the case for change simply by pointing to the numbers and insisting that the company achieve better ones. But messages communicated through numbers seldom stick. To the line managers—the very people the CEO needs to win over—the case for change seems abstract and remote. Those whose units are doing well feel that the criticism is not directed at them, that the problem is top management's. Managers of poorly performing units feel that they have been put on notice—and people worried about job security are more likely to be scanning the job market than trying to solve the company's problems.

Bratton in action

The New York Police Department was not Bill Bratton's first turnaround. The table describes his biggest challenges and achievements during his 20 years as a policy reformer.

Domain	Boston Police District 4	Massachusetts Bay Transit Authority (MBTA)	Boston Metropolitan Police ("The Mets")	New York Transit Police (NYTP)	New York Police Department (NYPD)
Years	1977–1982	1983–1986	1986–1990	1990–1992	1994–1996
Position	Sergeant, lieutenant	Superintendent	Superintendent	Chief of police	Commissioner
Setting	Assaults, drug dealing, prostitution, public drinking, and graffiti were endemic to the area. The Boston public shied away from attending baseball games and other events and from shopping in the Fenway neighborhood for fear of being robbed or attacked or having their cars stolen.	Subway crime had been on the rise for the past five years. The media dubbed the Boston subway the Terror Train. The *Boston Globe* published a series on police incompetence in the MBTA.	The Mets lacked modern equipment, procedures, and discipline. Physical facilities were crumbling. Accountability, discipline, and morale were low in the 600-person Mets workforce.	Crime had risen 25% per year in the past three years—twice the overall rate for the city. Subway use by the public had declined sharply; polls indicated that New Yorkers considered the subway the most dangerous place in the city. There were 170,000 fare evaders per day, costing the city $80 million annually. Aggressive panhandling and vandalism were endemic. More than 5,000 people were living in the subway system.	The middle class was fleeing to the suburbs in search of a better quality of life. There was public despair in the face of the high crime rate. Crime was seen as part of a breakdown of social norms. The budget for policing was shrinking. The NYPD budget (aside from personnel) was being cut by 35%. The staff was demoralized and relatively underpaid.

Domain	Boston Police District 4	Massachusetts Bay Transit Authority (MBTA)	Boston Metropolitan Police ("The Mets")	New York Transit Police (NYTP)	New York Police Department (NYPD)
Results	Crime throughout the Fenway area was dramatically reduced. Tourists, residents, and investment returned as an entire area of the city rebounded.	Crime on the MBTA decreased by 27%; arrests rose to 1,600 per year from 600. The MBTA police met more than 800 standards of excellence to be accredited by the National Commission on Accreditation for Police Agencies. It was only the 13th police department in the country to meet this standard. Equipment acquired during his tenure: 55 new midsize cars, new uniforms, and new logos. Ridership began to grow.	Employee morale rose as Bratton instilled accountability, protocol, and pride. In three years, the Metropolitan Police changed from a dispirited, do-nothing, reactive organization with a poor self-image and an even worse public image to a very proud, proactive department. Equipment acquired during his tenure: 100 new vehicles, a helicopter, and a state-of-the-art radio system.	In two years, Bratton reduced felony crime by 22%, with robberies down by 40%. Increased confidence in the subway led to increased ridership. Fare evasion was cut in half. Equipment acquired during his tenure: a state-of-the-art communication system, advanced handguns for officers, and new patrol cars (the number of cars doubled).	Overall crime fell by 17%. Felony crime fell by 39%. Murders fell by 50%. Theft fell by 35% (robberies were down by one-third, burglaries by one-quarter). There were 200,000 fewer victims a year than in 1990. By the end of Bratton's tenure, the NYPD had a 73% positive rating, up from 37% four years earlier.

For all these reasons, tipping point leaders like Bratton do not rely on numbers to break through the organization's cognitive hurdles. Instead, they put their key managers face-to-face with the operational problems so that the managers cannot evade reality. Poor performance becomes something they witness rather than hear about. Communicating in this way means that the message—performance is poor and needs to be fixed—sticks with people, which is essential if they are to be convinced not only that a turnaround is necessary but that it is something they can achieve.

When Bratton first went to New York to head the transit police in April 1990, he discovered that none of the senior staff officers rode the subway. They commuted to work and traveled around in cars provided by the city. Comfortably removed from the facts of underground life—and reassured by statistics showing that only 3% of the city's major crimes were committed in the subway—the senior managers had little sensitivity to riders' widespread concern about safety. In order to shatter the staff's complacency, Bratton began requiring that all transit police officials—beginning with himself—ride the subway to work, to meetings, and at night. It was many staff officers' first occasion in years to share the ordinary citizen's subway experience and see the situation their subordinates were up against: jammed turnstiles, aggressive beggars, gangs of youths jumping turnstiles and jostling people on the platforms, winos and homeless people sprawled on benches. It was clear that even if few major crimes took place in the subway, the whole place reeked of fear and disorder. With that ugly reality staring them in the face, the transit force's senior managers could no longer deny the need for a change in their policing methods.

Bratton uses a similar approach to help sensitize his superiors to his problems. For instance, when he was running the police division of the Massachusetts Bay Transit Authority (MBTA), which runs the Boston-area subway and buses, the transit authority's board decided to purchase small squad cars that would be cheaper to buy and run. Instead of fighting the decision, Bratton invited the MBTA's general manager for a tour of the district. He picked him up in a small car just like the ones that were to be ordered. He jammed the seats

Tipping point leadership at a glance

Leaders like Bill Bratton use a four-step process to bring about rapid, dramatic, and lasting change with limited resources. The cognitive and resource hurdles shown here represent the obstacles that organizations face in reorienting and formulating strategy. The motivational and political hurdles prevent a strategy's rapid execution. Tipping all four hurdles leads to rapid strategy reorientation and execution. Overcoming these hurdles is, of course, a continuous process because the innovation of today soon becomes the conventional norm of tomorrow.

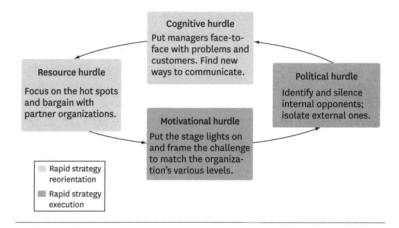

forward to let the general manager feel how little legroom a six-foot cop would have, then drove him over every pothole he could find. Bratton also put on his belt, cuffs, and gun for the trip so the general manager could see how little space there was for the tools of the officer's trade. After just two hours, the general manager wanted out. He said he didn't know how Bratton could stand being in such a cramped car for so long on his own—let alone if there were a criminal in the backseat. Bratton got the larger cars he wanted.

Bratton reinforces direct experiences by insisting that his officers meet the communities they are protecting. The feedback is often revealing. In the late 1970s, Boston's Police District 4, which included Symphony Hall, the Christian Science Mother Church, and other cultural institutions, was experiencing a surge in crime. The public was increasingly intimidated; residents were selling and leaving, pushing the community into a downward spiral. The Boston police performance statistics, however, did not reflect this reality. District 4 police, it seemed, were doing a splendid job of rapidly clearing 911 calls and tracking down perpetrators of serious crimes. To solve this paradox, Bratton had the unit organize community meetings in schoolrooms and civic centers so that citizens could voice their concerns to district sergeants and detectives. Obvious as the logic of this practice sounds, it was the first time in Boston's police history that anyone had attempted such an initiative—mainly because the practice up to that time had argued for detachment between police and the community in order to decrease the chances of police corruption.

The limitations of that practice quickly emerged. The meetings began with a show-and-tell by the officers: This is what we are working on and why. But afterward, when citizens were invited to discuss the issues that concerned them, a huge perception gap came to light. While the police officers took pride in solving serious offenses like grand larceny and murder, few citizens felt in any danger from these crimes. They were more troubled by constant minor irritants: prostitutes, panhandlers, broken-down cars left on the streets, drunks in the gutters, filth on the sidewalks. The town meetings quickly led to a complete overhaul of the police priorities for District 4. Bratton has used community meetings like this in every turnaround since.

Bratton's internal communications strategy also plays an important role in breaking through the cognitive hurdles. Traditionally, internal police communication is largely based on memos, staff bulletins, and other documents. Bratton knows that few police officers have the time or inclination to do more than throw these documents into the wastebasket. Officers rely instead on rumor and media stories for insights into what headquarters is up to. So Bratton typically calls on the help of expert communication outsiders. In New York, for instance, he recruited John Miller, an investigative television reporter known for his gutsy and innovative style, as his communication czar. Miller arranged for Bratton to communicate through video messages that were played at roll calls, which had the effect of bringing Bratton—and his opinions—closer to the people he had to win over. At the same time, Miller's journalistic savvy made it easier for the NYPD to ensure that press interviews and stories echoed the strong internal messages Bratton was sending.

Sidestep the Resource Hurdle

Once people in an organization accept the need for change and more or less agree on what needs to be done, leaders are often faced with the stark reality of limited resources. Do they have the money for the necessary changes? Most reformist CEOs do one of two things at this point. They trim their ambitions, dooming the company to mediocrity at best and demoralizing the workforce all over again, or they fight for more resources from their bankers and shareholders, a process that can take time and divert attention from the underlying problems.

That trap is completely avoidable. Leaders like Bratton know how to reach the organization's tipping point without extra resources. They can achieve a great deal with the resources they have. What they do is concentrate their resources on the places that are most in need of change and that have the biggest possible payoffs. This idea, in fact, is at the heart of Bratton's famous (and once hotly debated) philosophy of zero-tolerance policing.

Having won people over to the idea of change, Bratton must persuade them to take a cold look at what precisely is wrong with their operating practices. It is at this point that he turns to the numbers, which he is adept at using to force through major changes. Take the case of the New York narcotics unit. Bratton's predecessors had treated it as secondary in importance, partly because they assumed that responding to 911 calls was the top priority. As a result, less than 5% of the NYPD's manpower was dedicated to fighting narcotics crimes.

At an initial meeting with the NYPD's chiefs, Bratton's deputy commissioner of crime strategy, Jack Maple, asked people around the table for their estimates of the percentage of crimes attributable to narcotics use. Most said 50%; others, 70%; the lowest estimate was 30%. On that basis, a narcotics unit consisting of less than 5% of the police force was grossly understaffed, Maple pointed out. What's more, it turned out that the narcotics squad largely worked Monday through Friday, even though drugs were sold in large quantities—and drug-related crimes persistently occurred—on the weekends. Why the weekday schedule? Because it had always been done that way; it was an unquestioned modus operandi. Once these facts were presented, Bratton's call for a major reallocation of staff and resources within the NYPD was quickly accepted.

A careful examination of the facts can also reveal where changes in key policies can reduce the need for resources, as Bratton demonstrated during his tenure as chief of New York's transit police. His predecessors had lobbied hard for the money to increase the number of subway cops, arguing that the only way to stop muggers was to have officers ride every subway line and patrol each of the system's 700 exits and entrances. Bratton, by contrast, believed that subway crime could be resolved not by throwing more resources at the problem but by better targeting those resources. To prove the point, he had members of his staff analyze where subway crimes were being committed. They found that the vast majority occurred at only a few stations and on a couple of lines, which suggested that a targeted strategy would work well. At the same time, he shifted more of the force out of uniform and into plain clothes at the hot spots. Criminals soon realized that an absence of uniforms did not necessarily mean an absence of cops.

Distribution of officers was not the only problem. Bratton's analysis revealed that an inordinate amount of police time was wasted in processing arrests. It took an officer up to 16 hours per arrest to book the suspect and file papers on the incident. What's more, the officers so hated the bureaucratic process that they avoided making arrests in minor cases. Bratton realized that he could dramatically increase his available policing resources—not to mention the officers' motivation—if he could somehow improvise around this problem. His solution was to park "bust buses"—old buses converted into arrest-processing centers—around the corner from targeted subway stations. Processing time was cut from 16 hours to just one. Innovations like that enabled Bratton to dramatically reduce subway crime—even without an increase in the number of officers on duty at any given time. (The figure "The strategy canvas of transit: How Bratton refocused resources" illustrates how radically Bratton refocused the transit police's resources.)

Bratton's drive for data-driven policing solutions led to the creation of the famous Compstat crime database. The database, used to identify hot spots for intense police intervention, captures weekly crime and arrest activity—including times, locations, and associated enforcement activities—at the precinct, borough, and city levels. The Compstat reports allowed Bratton and the entire police department to easily discern established and emerging hot spots for efficient resource targeting and retargeting.

In addition to refocusing the resources he already controls, Bratton has proved adept at trading resources he doesn't need for those he does. The chiefs of public-sector organizations are reluctant to advertise excess resources, let alone lend them to other agencies, because acknowledged excess resources tend to get reallocated. So over time, some organizations end up well endowed with resources they don't need—even if they are short of others. When Bratton took over as chief of the transit police, for example, his general counsel and policy adviser, Dean Esserman, now police chief of Providence, Rhode Island, discovered that the transit unit had more unmarked cars than it needed but was starved of office space. The New York Division of Parole, on the other hand, was short of cars but had excess office space. Esserman and Bratton offered the obvious trade. It was gratefully accepted by the parole division, and transit officials were delighted to get the first floor of a prime downtown building. The deal stoked Bratton's credibility within the organization, which would make it easier for him to introduce more fundamental changes later, and it marked him, to his political bosses, as a man who could solve problems.

Jump the Motivational Hurdle

Alerting employees to the need for change and identifying how it can be achieved with limited resources are necessary for reaching an organization's tipping point. But if a new strategy is to become

The strategy canvas of transit:

How Bratton refocused resources

In comparing strategies across companies, we like to use a tool we call the strategy canvas, which highlights differences in strategies and resource allocation. The strategy canvas shown here compares the strategy and allocation of resources of the New York Transit Police before and after Bill Bratton's appointment as chief. The vertical axis shows the relative level of resource allocation. The horizontal axis shows the various elements of strategy in which the investments were made. Although a dramatic shift in resource allocation occurred and performance rose dramatically, overall investment of resources remained more or less constant. Bratton did this by de-emphasizing or virtually eliminating some traditional features of transit police work while increasing emphasis on others or creating new ones. For example, he was able to reduce the time police officers spent processing suspects by introducing mobile processing centers known as "bust buses."

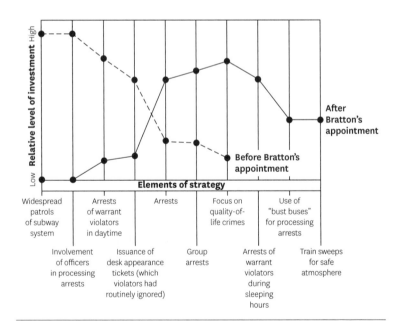

a movement, employees must not only recognize what needs to be done, they must also want to do it. Many CEOs recognize the importance of getting people motivated to make changes, but they make the mistake of trying to reform incentives throughout the whole organization. That process takes a long time to implement and can prove very expensive, given the wide variety of motivational needs in any large company.

One way Bratton solves the motivation problem is by singling out the key influencers—people inside or outside the organization with disproportionate power due to their connections with the organization, their ability to persuade, or their ability to block access to resources. Bratton recognizes that these influencers act like kingpins in bowling: When you hit them just right, all the pins topple over. Getting the key influencers motivated frees an organization from having to motivate everyone, yet everyone in the end is touched and changed. And because most organizations have relatively small numbers of key influencers, and those people tend to share common problems and concerns, it is relatively easy for CEOs to identify and motivate them.

Bratton's approach to motivating his key influencers is to put them under a spotlight. Perhaps his most significant reform of the NYPD's operating practices was instituting a semiweekly strategy review meeting that brought the top brass together with the city's 76 precinct commanders. Bratton had identified the commanders as key influential people in the NYPD, because each one directly managed 200 to 400 officers. Attendance was mandatory for all senior staff, including three-star chiefs, deputy commissioners, and borough chiefs. Bratton was there as often as possible.

At the meetings, which took place in an auditorium at the police command center, a selected precinct commander was called before a panel of the senior staff (the selected officer was given only two days' notice, in order to keep all the commanders on their toes). The commander in the spotlight was questioned by both the panel and other commanders about the precinct's performance. He or she was responsible for explaining projected maps and charts that showed, based on the Compstat data, the precinct's patterns of crimes and when and where the police responded. The commander would be required to provide a detailed explanation if police activity did not mirror crime spikes and would also be asked how officers were addressing the precinct's issues and why performance was improving or deteriorating. The meetings allowed Bratton and his senior staff to carefully monitor and assess how well commanders were motivating and managing their people and how well they were focusing on strategic hot spots.

The meetings changed the NYPD's culture in several ways. By making results and responsibilities clear to everyone, the meetings helped to introduce a culture of performance. Indeed, a photo of the commander who was about to be grilled appeared on the front page of the handout that each meeting participant received, emphasizing that the commander was accountable for the precinct's results. An incompetent commander could no longer cover up his failings by blaming his precinct's results on the shortcomings of neighboring precincts, because his neighbors were in the room and could respond. By the same token, the meetings gave high achievers a chance to be recognized both for making improvements in their own precincts and for helping other commanders. The meetings also allowed police leaders to compare notes on their experiences; before Bratton's arrival, precinct commanders hardly ever got together as a group. Over time, this management style filtered down through the ranks, as the precinct commanders tried out their own versions of Bratton's meetings. With the spotlight shining brightly on their performance, the commanders were highly motivated to get all the officers under their control marching to the new strategy.

The great challenges in applying this kind of motivational device, of course, are ensuring that people feel it is based on fair processes and seeing to it that they can draw lessons from both good and bad results. Doing so increases the organization's collective strength and everyone's chance of winning. Bratton addresses the issue of fair process by engaging all key influencers in the procedures, setting clear performance expectations, and explaining why these strategy meetings, for example, are essential for fast execution of policy. He addresses the issue of learning by insisting that the team of top brass play an active role in meetings and by being an active moderator himself. Precinct commanders can talk about their achievements or failures without feeling that they are showing off or being shown up. Successful commanders aren't seen as bragging, because it's clear to everyone that they were asked by Bratton's top team to show, in detail, how they achieved their successes. And for commanders on the receiving end, the sting of having to be taught a lesson by a colleague is mitigated, at least, by their not having to suffer the indignity of asking for it. Bratton's popularity soared when he created a humorous video satirizing the grilling that precinct commanders were given; it showed the cops that he understood just how much he was asking of them.

Bratton also uses another motivational lever: framing the reform challenge itself. Framing the challenge is one of the most subtle and sensitive tasks of the tipping point leader; unless people believe that results are attainable, a turnaround is unlikely to succeed. On the face of it, Bratton's goal in New York was so ambitious as to be scarcely believable. Who would believe that the city could be made one of the safest in the country? And who would want to invest time and energy in chasing such an impossible dream?

To make the challenge seem manageable, Bratton framed it as a series of specific goals that officers at different levels could relate to. As he put it, the challenge the NYPD faced was to make the streets of New York safe "block by block, precinct by precinct, and borough by borough." Thus framed, the task was both all encompassing and doable. For the cops on the street, the challenge was making their beats or blocks safe—no more. For the commanders, the challenge was making their precincts safe—no more. Borough heads also had a concrete goal within their capabilities: making their boroughs safe—no more. No matter what their positions, officers couldn't say that what was being asked of them was too tough. Nor could they claim that achieving it was out of their hands. In this way, responsibility for the turnaround shifted from Bratton to each of the thousands of police officers on the force.

Knock Over the Political Hurdle

Organizational politics is an inescapable reality in public and corporate life, a lesson Bratton learned the hard way. In 1980, at age 34 one of the youngest lieutenants in Boston's police department, he had proudly put up a plaque in his office that said: "Youth and skill will win out every time over age and treachery." Within just a few months, having been shunted into a dead-end position due to a mixture of office politics and his own brashness, Bratton took the sign down. He never again forgot the importance of understanding the plotting, intrigue, and politics involved in pushing through change. Even if an organization has reached the tipping point, powerful vested interests will resist the impending reforms. The more likely change becomes, the more fiercely and vocally these negative influencers—both internal and external—will fight to protect their positions, and their resistance can seriously damage, even derail, the reform process.

Bratton anticipates these dangers by identifying and silencing powerful naysayers early on. To that end, he always ensures that he has a respected senior insider on the top team. At the NYPD, for instance, Bratton appointed John Timoney, now Miami's police commissioner, as his number two. Timoney was a cop's cop, respected and feared for his dedication to the NYPD and for the more than 60 decorations he had received. Twenty years in the ranks had taught him who all the key players were and how they played the political game. One of the first tasks Timoney carried out was to report to Bratton on the likely attitudes of the top staff toward Bratton's concept of zero-tolerance policing, identifying those who would fight or silently sabotage the new initiatives. This led to a dramatic changing of the guard.

Of course, not all naysayers should face the ultimate sanction—there might not be enough people left to man the barricades. In many cases, therefore, Bratton silences opposition by example and indisputable fact. For instance, when first asked to compile detailed crime maps and information packages for the strategy review meetings, most precinct commanders complained that the task would take too long and waste valuable police time that could be better spent fighting crime. Anticipating this argument, deputy commissioner Jack Maple set up a reporting system that covered the city's most crime-ridden areas. Operating the system required no more than 18 minutes a day, which worked out, as he told the precinct commanders, to less than 1% of the average precinct's workload. Try to argue with that.

Often the most serious opposition to reform comes from outside. In the public sector, as in business, an organization's change of strategy has an impact on other organizations—partners and competitors alike. The change is likely to be resisted by those players if they are happy with the status quo and powerful enough to protest the changes. Bratton's strategy for dealing with such opponents is to isolate them by building a broad coalition with the other independent powers in his realm. In New York, for example, one of the most serious threats to his reforms came from the city's courts, which were concerned that zero-tolerance policing would result in an enormous number of small-crimes cases clogging the court schedule.

To get past the opposition of the courts, Bratton solicited the support of no less a personage than the mayor, Rudolph Giuliani, who had considerable influence over the district attorneys, the courts, and the city jail on Rikers Island. Bratton's team demonstrated to the mayor that the court system had the capacity to handle minor "quality of life" crimes, even though doing so would presumably not be palatable for them.

The mayor decided to intervene. While conceding to the courts that a crackdown campaign would cause a short-term spike in court work, he also made clear that he and the NYPD believed it would eventually lead to a workload reduction for the courts. Working together in this way, Bratton and the mayor were able to maneuver the courts into processing quality-of-life crimes. Seeing that the mayor was aligned with Bratton, the courts appealed to the city's legislators, advocating legislation to exempt them from handling minor-crime cases on the grounds that such cases would clog the system and entail significant costs to the city. Bratton and the mayor, who were holding weekly strategy meetings, added another ally to their coalition by placing their case before the press, in particular the *New York Times.* Through a series of press conferences and articles and at every interview opportunity, the issue of zero tolerance was put at the front and center of public debate with a clear, simple message: If the courts did not help crack down on quality-of-life crimes, the city's crime rates would not improve. It was a matter not of saving dollars but of saving the city.

Bratton's alliance with the mayor's office and the city's leading media institution successfully isolated the courts. The courts could hardly be seen as publicly opposing an initiative that would not only make New York a more attractive place to live but would ultimately reduce the number of cases brought before them. With the mayor speaking aggressively in the press about the need to pursue quality-of-life crimes and the city's most respected—and liberal—newspaper giving credence to the policy, the costs of fighting Bratton's strategy were daunting. Thanks to this savvy politicking, one of Bratton's biggest battles was won, and the legislation was not enacted. The courts would handle quality-of-life crimes. In due course, the crime rates did indeed come tumbling down.

———————————————

Of course, Bill Bratton, like any leader, must share the credit for his successes. Turning around an organization as large and as wedded to the status quo as the NYPD requires a collective effort. But the tipping point would not have been reached without him—or another leader like him. And while we recognize that not every executive has the personality to be a Bill Bratton, there are many who have that potential once they know the formula for success. It is that formula that we have tried to present, and we urge managers who wish to turn their companies around, but have limited time and resources, to take note. By addressing the hurdles to tipping point change described in these pages, they will stand a chance of achieving the same kind of results for their shareholders as Bratton has delivered to the citizens of New York.

Originally published in April 2003. Reprint R0304D

Blue Ocean Strategy

A ONETIME ACCORDION PLAYER, stilt walker, and fire-eater, Guy Laliberté is now CEO of one of Canada's largest cultural exports, Cirque du Soleil. Founded in 1984 by a group of street performers, Cirque has staged dozens of productions seen by some 40 million people in 90 cities around the world. In 20 years, Cirque has achieved revenues that Ringling Bros. and Barnum & Bailey—the world's leading circus—took more than a century to attain.

Cirque's rapid growth occurred in an unlikely setting. The circus business was (and still is) in long-term decline. Alternative forms of entertainment—sporting events, TV, and video games—were casting a growing shadow. Children, the mainstay of the circus audience, preferred PlayStations to circus acts. There was also rising sentiment, fueled by animal rights groups, against the use of animals, traditionally an integral part of the circus. On the supply side, the star performers that Ringling and the other circuses relied on to draw in the crowds could often name their own terms. As a result, the industry was hit by steadily decreasing audiences and increasing costs. What's more, any new entrant to this business would be competing against a formidable incumbent that for most of the last century had set the industry standard.

How did Cirque profitably increase revenues by a factor of 22 over the last ten years in such an unattractive environment? The tagline for one of the first Cirque productions is revealing: "We reinvent the circus." Cirque did not make its money by competing within the confines of the existing industry or by stealing customers from Ringling and the others. Instead it created uncontested market space that made the competition irrelevant. It pulled in a whole new group of customers who were traditionally noncustomers of the industry—adults and corporate clients who had turned to theater, opera, or ballet and were, therefore, prepared to pay several times more than the price of a conventional circus ticket for an unprecedented entertainment experience.

To understand the nature of Cirque's achievement, you have to realize that the business universe consists of two distinct kinds of space, which we think of as red and blue oceans. Red oceans represent all the industries in existence today—the known market space. In red oceans, industry boundaries are defined and accepted, and the competitive rules of the game are well understood. Here, companies try to outperform their rivals in order to grab a greater share of existing demand. As the space gets more and more crowded, prospects for profits and growth are reduced. Products turn into commodities, and increasing competition turns the water bloody.

Blue oceans denote all the industries *not* in existence today—the unknown market space, untainted by competition. In blue oceans, demand is created rather than fought over. There is ample opportunity for growth that is both profitable and rapid. There are two ways to create blue oceans. In a few cases, companies can give rise to completely new industries, as eBay did with the online auction industry. But in most cases, a blue ocean is created from within a red ocean when a company alters the boundaries of an existing industry. As will become evident later, this is what Cirque did. In breaking through the boundary traditionally separating circus and theater, it made a new and profitable blue ocean from within the red ocean of the circus industry.

Cirque is just one of more than 150 blue ocean creations that we have studied in over 30 industries, using data stretching back more than 100 years. We analyzed companies that created those blue oceans and their less successful competitors, which were caught in red oceans. In studying these data, we have observed a consistent pattern of strategic thinking behind the creation of new markets and industries, what we call blue ocean strategy. The logic behind blue ocean strategy parts with traditional models focused on competing

Idea in Brief

The best way to drive profitable growth? Stop competing in over-crowded industries. In those **red oceans**, companies try to outperform rivals to grab bigger slices of existing demand. As the space gets increasingly crowded, profit and growth prospects shrink. Products become commoditized. Ever-more-intense competition turns the water bloody.

How to avoid the fray? Kim and Mauborgne recommend creating **blue oceans**—uncontested market spaces where the competition is irrelevant. In blue oceans, you invent and capture new demand,

and you offer customers a leap in value while also streamlining your costs. Results? Handsome profits, speedy growth—and brand equity that lasts for decades while rivals scramble to catch up.

Consider Cirque du Soleil—which invented a new industry that combined elements from traditional circus with elements drawn from sophisticated theater. In just 20 years, Cirque raked in revenues that Ringling Bros. and Barnum & Bailey—the world's leading circus—needed more than a century to attain.

in existing market space. Indeed, it can be argued that managers' failure to realize the differences between red and blue ocean strategy lies behind the difficulties many companies encounter as they try to break from the competition.

In this article, we present the concept of blue ocean strategy and describe its defining characteristics. We assess the profit and growth consequences of blue oceans and discuss why their creation is a rising imperative for companies in the future. We believe that an understanding of blue ocean strategy will help today's companies as they struggle to thrive in an accelerating and expanding business universe.

Blue and Red Oceans

Although the term may be new, blue oceans have always been with us. Look back 100 years and ask yourself which industries known today were then unknown. The answer: Industries as basic as automobiles, music recording, aviation, petrochemicals, pharmaceuticals,

Idea in Practice

How to begin creating blue oceans? Kim and Mauborgne offer these suggestions:

Understand the Logic Behind Blue Ocean Strategy

The logic behind blue ocean strategy is counterintuitive:

- **It's not about technology innovation.** Blue oceans seldom result from technological innovation. Often, the underlying technology already exists—and blue ocean creators link it to what buyers value. Compaq, for example, used existing technologies to create its ProSignia server, which gave buyers twice the file and print capability of the minicomputer at one-third the price.

- **You don't have to venture into distant waters to create blue oceans.** Most blue oceans are created from within, not beyond, the red oceans of existing industries. Incumbents often create blue oceans within their core businesses. Consider the megaplexes introduced by AMC—an established player in the movie-theater industry. Megaplexes provided moviegoers spectacular viewing experiences in stadium-size theater complexes at lower costs to theater owners.

Apply Blue Ocean Strategic Moves

To apply blue ocean strategic moves:

- **Never use the competition as a benchmark.** Instead, make

and management consulting were unheard-of or had just begun to emerge. Now turn the clock back only 30 years and ask yourself the same question. Again, a plethora of multibillion-dollar industries jump out: mutual funds, cellular telephones, biotechnology, discount retailing, express package delivery, snowboards, coffee bars, and home videos, to name a few. Just three decades ago, none of these industries existed in a meaningful way.

This time, put the clock forward 20 years. Ask yourself: How many industries that are unknown today will exist then? If history is any predictor of the future, the answer is many. Companies have a huge capacity to create new industries and re-create existing ones, a fact that is reflected in the deep changes that have been necessary in the way industries are classified. The half-century-old Standard Industrial Classification (SIC) system was replaced in 1997

the competition irrelevant by creating a leap in value for both yourself and your customers. Ford did this with the Model T. Ford could have tried besting the fashionable, customized cars that wealthy people bought for weekend jaunts in the countryside. Instead, it offered a car for everyday use that was far more affordable, durable, and easy to use and fix than rivals' offerings. Model T sales boomed, and Ford's market share surged from 9% in 1908 to 61% in 1921.

- **Reduce your costs while also offering customers more value.** Cirque du Soleil omitted costly elements of traditional circus, such as animal acts and aisle concessions. Its reduced cost structure enabled it to provide sophisticated elements from theater that appealed to adult audiences—such as themes, original scores, and enchanting sets, all of which change year to year. The added value lured adults who had not gone to a circus for years and enticed them to come back more frequently—thereby increasing revenues. By offering the best of circus and theater, Cirque created a market space that, as yet, has no name—and no equals.

by the North American Industry Classification System (NAICS). The new system expanded the ten SIC industry sectors into 20 to reflect the emerging realities of new industry territories—blue oceans. The services sector under the old system, for example, is now seven sectors ranging from information to health care and social assistance. Given that these classification systems are designed for standardization and continuity, such a replacement shows how significant a source of economic growth the creation of blue oceans has been.

Looking forward, it seems clear to us that blue oceans will remain the engine of growth. Prospects in most established market spaces—red oceans—are shrinking steadily. Technological advances have substantially improved industrial productivity, permitting suppliers to produce an unprecedented array of products and services. And as trade barriers between nations and regions fall and information on products and prices becomes instantly and globally available, niche markets and monopoly havens are continuing to disappear. At the same time, there is little evidence of any increase in demand, at least in the developed markets, where recent United Nations statistics even point to declining populations. The result is that in more and more industries, supply is overtaking demand.

This situation has inevitably hastened the commoditization of products and services, stoked price wars, and shrunk profit margins. According to recent studies, major American brands in a variety of product and service categories have become more and more alike. And as brands become more similar, people increasingly base purchase choices on price. People no longer insist, as in the past, that their laundry detergent be Tide. Nor do they necessarily stick to Colgate when there is a special promotion for Crest, and vice versa. In overcrowded industries, differentiating brands becomes harder both in economic upturns and in downturns.

The Paradox of Strategy

Unfortunately, most companies seem becalmed in their red oceans. In a study of business launches in 108 companies, we found that 86% of those new ventures were line extensions—incremental improvements to existing industry offerings—and a mere 14% were aimed at creating new markets or industries. While line extensions did account for 62% of the total revenues, they delivered only 39% of the total profits. By contrast, the 14% invested in creating new markets and industries delivered 38% of total revenues and a startling 61% of total profits.

So why the dramatic imbalance in favor of red oceans? Part of the explanation is that corporate strategy is heavily influenced by its roots in military strategy. The very language of strategy is deeply imbued with military references—chief executive "officers" in "headquarters," "troops" on the "front lines." Described this way, strategy is all about red ocean competition. It is about confronting an opponent and driving him off a battlefield of limited territory. Blue ocean strategy, by contrast, is about doing business where there is no competitor. It is about creating new land, not dividing up existing land. Focusing on the red ocean therefore means accepting the key constraining factors of war—limited terrain and the need to beat an enemy to succeed. And it means denying the distinctive strength of the business world—the capacity to create new market space that is uncontested.

The tendency of corporate strategy to focus on winning against rivals was exacerbated by the meteoric rise of Japanese companies in the 1970s and 1980s. For the first time in corporate history, customers were deserting Western companies in droves. As competition mounted in the global marketplace, a slew of red ocean strategies emerged, all arguing that competition was at the core of corporate success and failure. Today, one hardly talks about strategy without using the language of competition. The term that best symbolizes this is "competitive advantage." In the competitive-advantage worldview, companies are often driven to outperform rivals and capture greater shares of existing market space.

Of course competition matters. But by focusing on competition, scholars, companies, and consultants have ignored two very important—and, we would argue, far more lucrative—aspects of strategy: One is to find and develop markets where there is little or no competition—blue oceans—and the other is to exploit and protect blue oceans. These challenges are very different from those to which strategists have devoted most of their attention.

Toward Blue Ocean Strategy

What kind of strategic logic is needed to guide the creation of blue oceans? To answer that question, we looked back over 100 years of data on blue ocean creation to see what patterns could be discerned. Some of our data are presented in "A snapshot of blue ocean creation." It shows an overview of key blue ocean creations in three industries that closely touch people's lives: autos—how people get to work; computers—what people use at work; and movie theaters—where people go after work for enjoyment. We found that:

A snapshot of blue ocean creation

This table identifies the strategic elements that were common to blue ocean creations in three different industries in different eras. It is not intended to be comprehensive in coverage or exhaustive in content. We chose to show American industries because they represented the largest and least-regulated market during our study period. The pattern of blue ocean creations exemplified by these three industries is consistent with what we observed in the other industries in our study.

Key blue ocean creations	Was the blue ocean created by a new entrant or an incumbent?	Was it driven by technology pioneering or value pioneering?	At the time of the blue ocean creation, was the industry attractive or unattractive?
Automobiles			
Ford Model T Unveiled in 1908, the Model T was the first mass-produced car, priced so that many Americans could afford it.	New entrant	Value pioneering* (mostly existing technologies)	Unattractive
GM's "car for every purse and purpose" GM created a blue ocean in 1924 by injecting fun and fashion into the car.	Incumbent	Value pioneering (some new technologies)	Attractive
Japanese fuel-efficient autos Japanese automakers created a blue ocean in the mid-1970s with small, reliable lines of cars.	Incumbent	Value pioneering (some new technologies)	Unattractive
Chrysler minivan With its 1984 minivan, Chrysler created a new class of automobile that was as easy to use as a car but had the passenger space of a van.	Incumbent	Value pioneering (mostly existing technologies)	Unattractive

Key blue ocean creations	Was the blue ocean created by a new entrant or an incumbent?	Was it driven by technology pioneering or value pioneering?	At the time of the blue ocean creation, was the industry attractive or unattractive?
Computers			
CTR's tabulating machine In 1914, CTR created the business machine industry by simplifying, modularizing, and leasing tabulating machines. CTR later changed its name to IBM.	Incumbent	Value pioneering (some new technologies)	Unattractive
IBM 650 electronic computer and System/360 In 1952, IBM created the business computer industry by simplifying and reducing the power and price of existing technology. And it exploded the blue ocean created by the 650 when in 1964 it unveiled the System/360, the first modularized computer system.	Incumbent	Value pioneering (650: mostly existing technologies) Value and technology pioneering (System/360: new and existing technologies)	Nonexistent
Apple personal computer Although it was not the first home computer, the all-in-one, simple-to-use Apple II was a blue ocean creation when it appeared in 1978.	New entrant	Value pioneering (mostly existing technologies)	Unattractive
Compaq PC servers Compaq created a blue ocean in 1992 with its ProSignia server, which gave buyers twice the file and print capability of the minicomputer at one-third the price.	Incumbent	Value pioneering (mostly existing technologies)	Nonexistent

(continued)

Key blue ocean creations	Was the blue ocean created by a new entrant or an incumbent?	Was it driven by technology pioneering or value pioneering?	At the time of the blue ocean creation, was the industry attractive or unattractive?
Dell built-to-order computers In the mid-1990s, Dell created a blue ocean in a highly competitive industry by creating a new purchase and delivery experience for buyers.	New entrant	Value pioneering (mostly existing technologies)	Unattractive
Movie theaters			
Nickelodeon The first Nickelodeon opened its doors in 1905, showing short films around-the-clock to working-class audiences for five cents.	New entrant	Value pioneering (mostly existing technologies)	Nonexistent
Palace theaters Created by Roxy Rothapfel in 1914, these theaters pro-vided an operalike environ-ment for cinema viewing at an affordable price.	Incumbent	Value pioneering (mostly existing technologies)	Attractive
AMC multiplex In the 1960s, the number of multiplexes in America's suburban shopping malls mushroomed. The multi-plex gave viewers greater choice while reducing owners' costs.	Incumbent	Value pioneering (mostly existing technologies)	Unattractive
AMC megaplex Megaplexes, introduced in 1995, offered every current blockbuster and provided spectacular viewing ex-periences in theater com-plexes as big as stadiums, at a lower cost to theater owners.	Incumbent	Value pioneering (mostly existing technologies)	Unattractive

*Driven by value pioneering does not mean that technologies were not involved. Rather, it means that the defining technologies used had largely been in existence, whether in that industry or elsewhere.

Blue oceans are not about technology innovation

Leading-edge technology is sometimes involved in the creation of blue oceans, but it is not a defining feature of them. This is often true even in industries that are technology intensive. As the exhibit reveals, across all three representative industries, blue oceans were seldom the result of technological innovation per se; the underlying technology was often already in existence. Even Ford's revolutionary assembly line can be traced to the meatpacking industry in America. Like those within the auto industry, the blue oceans within the computer industry did not come about through technology innovations alone but by linking technology to what buyers valued. As with the IBM 650 and the Compaq PC server, this often involved simplifying the technology.

Incumbents often create blue oceans—and usually within their core businesses

GM, the Japanese automakers, and Chrysler were established players when they created blue oceans in the auto industry. So were CTR and its later incarnation, IBM, and Compaq in the computer industry. And in the cinema industry, the same can be said of palace theaters and AMC. Of the companies listed here, only Ford, Apple, Dell, and Nickelodeon were new entrants in their industries; the first three were start-ups, and the fourth was an established player entering an industry that was new to it. This suggests that incumbents are not at a disadvantage in creating new market spaces. Moreover, the blue oceans made by incumbents were usually within their core businesses. In fact, as the exhibit shows, most blue oceans are created from within, not beyond, red oceans of existing industries. This challenges the view that new markets are in distant waters. Blue oceans are right next to you in every industry.

Company and industry are the wrong units of analysis

The traditional units of strategic analysis—company and industry—have little explanatory power when it comes to analyzing how and why blue oceans are created. There is no consistently excellent company; the same company can be brilliant at one time and wrong-headed at another. Every company rises and falls over time. Likewise, there is no perpetually excellent industry; relative attractiveness is driven largely by the creation of blue oceans from within them.

The most appropriate unit of analysis for explaining the creation of blue oceans is the strategic move—the set of managerial actions and decisions involved in making a major market-creating business offering. Compaq, for example, is considered by many people to be "unsuccessful" because it was acquired by Hewlett-Packard in 2001 and ceased to be a company. But the firm's ultimate fate does not invalidate the smart strategic move Compaq made that led to the creation of the multibillion-dollar market in PC servers, a move that was a key cause of the company's powerful comeback in the 1990s.

Creating blue oceans builds brands

So powerful is blue ocean strategy that a blue ocean strategic move can create brand equity that lasts for decades. Almost all of the companies listed in the exhibit are remembered in no small part for the blue oceans they created long ago. Very few people alive today were around when the first Model T rolled off Henry Ford's assembly line in 1908, but the company's brand still benefits from that blue ocean move. IBM, too, is often regarded as an "American institution" largely for the blue oceans it created in computing; the 360 series was its equivalent of the Model T.

Our findings are encouraging for executives at the large, established corporations that are traditionally seen as the victims of new market space creation. For what they reveal is that large R&D budgets are not the key to creating new market space. The key is making the right strategic moves. What's more, companies that understand what drives a good strategic move will be well placed to create multiple blue oceans over time, thereby continuing to deliver high growth and profits over a sustained period. The creation of blue oceans, in other words, is a product of strategy and as such is very much a product of managerial action.

The Defining Characteristics

Our research shows several common characteristics across strategic moves that create blue oceans. We found that the creators of blue oceans, in sharp contrast to companies playing by traditional rules, never use the competition as a benchmark. Instead they make it irrelevant by creating a leap in value for both buyers and the company itself. (The exhibit "Red ocean versus blue ocean strategy" compares the chief characteristics of these two strategy models.)

Perhaps the most important feature of blue ocean strategy is that it rejects the fundamental tenet of conventional strategy: that a trade-off exists between value and cost. According to this thesis, companies can either create greater value for customers at a higher cost or create reasonable value at a lower cost. In other words, strategy is essentially a choice between differentiation and low cost. But when it comes to creating blue oceans, the evidence shows that successful companies pursue differentiation and low cost simultaneously.

To see how this is done, let us go back to Cirque du Soleil. At the time of Cirque's debut, circuses focused on benchmarking one another and maximizing their shares of shrinking demand by tweaking traditional circus acts. This included trying to secure more and better-known clowns and lion tamers, efforts that raised circuses' cost structure without substantially altering the circus experience. The result was rising costs without rising revenues and a downward spiral in overall circus demand. Enter Cirque. Instead of following the conventional logic of outpacing the competition by offering a better solution to the given problem—creating a circus with even greater fun and thrills—it redefined the problem itself by offering people the fun and thrill of the circus *and* the intellectual sophistication and artistic richness of the theater.

In designing performances that landed both these punches, Cirque had to reevaluate the components of the traditional circus offering. What the company found was that many of the elements considered essential to the fun and thrill of the circus were unnecessary and in many cases costly. For instance, most circuses offer animal acts. These are a heavy economic burden, because circuses have to

Red ocean versus blue ocean strategy

The imperatives for red ocean and blue ocean strategies are starkly different.

Red ocean strategy	Blue ocean strategy
Compete in existing market space.	Create uncontested market space.
Beat the competition.	Make the competition irrelevant.
Exploit existing demand.	Create and capture new demand.
Make the value/cost trade-off.	Break the value/cost trade-off.
Align the whole system of a company's activities with its strategic choice of differentiation or low cost.	Align the whole system of a company's activities in pursuit of differentiation and low cost.

shell out not only for the animals but also for their training, medical care, housing, insurance, and transportation. Yet Cirque found that the appetite for animal shows was rapidly diminishing because of rising public concern about the treatment of circus animals and the ethics of exhibiting them.

Similarly, although traditional circuses promoted their performers as stars, Cirque realized that the public no longer thought of circus artists as stars, at least not in the movie star sense. Cirque did away with traditional three-ring shows, too. Not only did these create confusion among spectators forced to switch their attention from one ring to another, they also increased the number of performers needed, with obvious cost implications. And while aisle concession sales appeared to be a good way to generate revenue, the high prices discouraged parents from making purchases and made them feel they were being taken for a ride.

Cirque found that the lasting allure of the traditional circus came down to just three factors: the clowns, the tent, and the classic acrobatic acts. So Cirque kept the clowns, while shifting their humor away from slapstick to a more enchanting, sophisticated style. It glamorized the tent, which many circuses had abandoned in favor of rented venues. Realizing that the tent, more than anything else, captured the magic of the circus, Cirque designed this classic symbol with a glorious external finish and a high level of audience comfort. Gone were the sawdust and hard benches. Acrobats and other thrilling performers were retained, but Cirque reduced their roles and made their acts more elegant by adding artistic flair.

Even as Cirque stripped away some of the traditional circus offerings, it injected new elements drawn from the world of theater. For instance, unlike traditional circuses featuring a series of unrelated acts, each Cirque creation resembles a theater performance in that it has a theme and story line. Although the themes are intentionally vague, they bring harmony and an intellectual element to the acts. Cirque also borrows ideas from Broadway. For example, rather than putting on the traditional "once and for all" show, Cirque mounts multiple productions based on different themes and story lines. As with Broadway productions, too, each Cirque show has an original musical score, which drives the performance, lighting, and timing of the acts, rather than the other way around. The productions feature abstract and spiritual dance, an idea derived from theater and ballet. By introducing these factors, Cirque has created highly sophisticated entertainments. And by staging multiple productions, Cirque gives people reason to come to the circus more often, thereby increasing revenues.

Cirque offers the best of both circus and theater. And by eliminating many of the most expensive elements of the circus, it has been able to dramatically reduce its cost structure, achieving both differentiation and low cost. (For a depiction of the economics underpinning blue ocean strategy, see "The simultaneous pursuit of differentiation and low cost.")

By driving down costs while simultaneously driving up value for buyers, a company can achieve a leap in value for both itself and its customers. Since buyer value comes from the utility and price a company offers, and a company generates value for itself through cost structure and price, blue ocean strategy is achieved only when the whole system of a company's utility, price, and cost activities is properly aligned. It is this whole-system approach that makes the creation of blue oceans a sustainable strategy. Blue ocean strategy integrates the range of a firm's functional and operational activities.

A rejection of the trade-off between low cost and differentiation implies a fundamental change in strategic mind-set—we cannot emphasize enough how fundamental a shift it is. The red ocean assumption that industry structural conditions are a given and firms are forced to compete within them is based on an intellectual worldview that academics call the *structuralist* view, or *environmental determinism*. According to this view, companies and managers are largely at the mercy of economic forces greater than themselves. Blue ocean strategies, by contrast, are based on a worldview in which market boundaries and industries can be reconstructed by the actions and beliefs of industry players. We call this the *reconstructionist* view.

The founders of Cirque du Soleil clearly did not feel constrained to act within the confines of their industry. Indeed, is Cirque really a circus with all that it has eliminated, reduced, raised, and created? Or is it theater? If it is theater, then what genre—Broadway show, opera, ballet? The magic of Cirque was created through a reconstruction of elements drawn from all of these alternatives. In the end, Cirque is none of them and a little of all of them. From within the red oceans of theater and circus, Cirque has created a blue ocean of uncontested market space that has, as yet, no name.

Barriers to Imitation

Companies that create blue oceans usually reap the benefits without credible challenges for ten to 15 years, as was the case with Cirque du Soleil, Home Depot, Federal Express, Southwest Airlines, and CNN, to name just a few. The reason is that blue ocean strategy creates considerable economic and cognitive barriers to imitation.

For a start, adopting a blue ocean creator's business model is easier to imagine than to do. Because blue ocean creators immediately attract customers in large volumes, they are able to generate scale economies very rapidly, putting would-be imitators at an immediate and continuing cost disadvantage. The huge economies of scale

The simultaneous pursuit of differentiation and low cost

A blue ocean is created in the region where a company's actions favorably affect both its cost structure and its value proposition to buyers. Cost savings are made from eliminating and reducing the factors an industry competes on. Buyer value is lifted by raising and creating elements the industry has never offered. Over time, costs are reduced further as scale economies kick in, due to the high sales volumes that superior value generates.

in purchasing that Wal-Mart enjoys, for example, have significantly discouraged other companies from imitating its business model. The immediate attraction of large numbers of customers can also create network externalities. The more customers eBay has online, the more attractive the auction site becomes for both sellers and buyers of wares, giving users few incentives to go elsewhere.

When imitation requires companies to make changes to their whole system of activities, organizational politics may impede a would-be competitor's ability to switch to the divergent business model of a blue ocean strategy. For instance, airlines trying to follow Southwest's example of offering the speed of air travel with the flexibility and cost of driving would have faced major revisions in routing, training, marketing, and pricing, not to mention culture. Few established airlines had the flexibility to make such extensive organizational and operating changes overnight. Imitating a whole-system approach is not an easy feat.

The cognitive barriers can be just as effective. When a company offers a leap in value, it rapidly earns brand buzz and a loyal following in the marketplace. Experience shows that even the most expensive marketing campaigns struggle to unseat a blue ocean creator. Microsoft, for example, has been trying for more than ten years to occupy the center of the blue ocean that Intuit created with its financial software product Quicken. Despite all of its efforts and all of its investment, Microsoft has not been able to unseat Intuit as the industry leader.

In other situations, attempts to imitate a blue ocean creator conflict with the imitator's existing brand image. The Body Shop, for example, shuns top models and makes no promises of eternal youth and beauty. For the established cosmetic brands like Estée Lauder and L'Oréal, imitation was very difficult, because it would have signaled a complete invalidation of their current images, which are based on promises of eternal youth and beauty.

A Consistent Pattern

While our conceptual articulation of the pattern may be new, blue ocean strategy has always existed, whether or not companies have been conscious of the fact. Just consider the striking parallels between the Cirque du Soleil theater-circus experience and Ford's creation of the Model T.

At the end of the nineteenth century, the automobile industry was small and unattractive. More than 500 automakers in America competed in turning out handmade luxury cars that cost around $1,500 and were enormously *un*popular with all but the very rich. Anticar activists tore up roads, ringed parked cars with barbed wire, and organized boycotts of car-driving businessmen and politicians. Woodrow Wilson caught the spirit of the times when he said in 1906 that "nothing has spread socialistic feeling more than the automobile." He called it "a picture of the arrogance of wealth."

Instead of trying to beat the competition and steal a share of existing demand from other automakers, Ford reconstructed the industry boundaries of cars and horse-drawn carriages to create a blue ocean. At the time, horse-drawn carriages were the primary means of local transportation across America. The carriage had two distinct advantages over cars. Horses could easily negotiate the bumps and mud that stymied cars—especially in rain and snow—on the nation's ubiquitous dirt roads. And horses and carriages were much easier to maintain than the luxurious autos of the time, which frequently broke down, requiring expert repairmen who were expensive and in short supply. It was Henry Ford's understanding of these advantages that showed him how he could break away from the competition and unlock enormous untapped demand.

Ford called the Model T the car "for the great multitude, constructed of the best materials." Like Cirque, the Ford Motor Company made the competition irrelevant. Instead of creating fashionable, custom-ized cars for weekends in the countryside, a luxury few could justify, Ford built a car that, like the horse-drawn carriage, was for everyday use. The Model T came in just one color, black, and there were few optional extras. It was reliable and durable, designed to travel effort-lessly over dirt roads in rain, snow, or sunshine. It was easy to use and fix. People could learn to drive it in a day. And like Cirque, Ford went outside the industry for a price point, looking at horse-drawn carriages ($400), not other autos. In 1908, the first Model T cost $850; in 1909, the price dropped to $609, and by 1924 it was down to $290. In this way, Ford converted buyers of horse-drawn carriages into car buyers—just as Cirque turned theatergoers into circusgoers. Sales of the Model T boomed. Ford's market share surged from 9% in 1908 to 61% in 1921, and by 1923, a majority of American households had a car.

Even as Ford offered the mass of buyers a leap in value, the com-pany also achieved the lowest cost structure in the industry, much as Cirque did later. By keeping the cars highly standardized with lim-ited options and interchangeable parts, Ford was able to scrap the prevailing manufacturing system in which cars were constructed by skilled craftsmen who swarmed around one workstation and built a car piece by piece from start to finish. Ford's revolutionary assem-bly line replaced craftsmen with unskilled laborers, each of whom worked quickly and efficiently on one small task. This allowed Ford to make a car in just four days—21 days was the industry norm—creating huge cost savings.

Blue and red oceans have always coexisted and always will. Practical reality, therefore, demands that companies understand the strategic logic of both types of oceans. At present, competing in red oceans dominates the field of strategy in theory and in practice, even as businesses' need to create blue oceans intensifies. It is time to even the scales in the field of strategy with a better balance of efforts across both oceans. For although blue ocean strategists have always existed, for the most part their strategies have been largely unconscious. But once corporations realize that the strategies for creating and capturing blue oceans have a different underlying logic from red ocean strategies, they will be able to create many more blue oceans in the future.

Originally published in October 2004. Reprint R0401D

How Strategy
Shapes Structure

WHEN EXECUTIVES DEVELOP CORPORATE STRATEGY, they nearly always begin by analyzing the industry or environmental conditions in which they operate. They then assess the strengths and weaknesses of the players they are up against. With these industry and competitive analyses in mind, they set out to carve a distinctive strategic position where they can outperform their rivals by building a competitive advantage. To obtain such advantage, a company generally chooses either to differentiate itself from the competition for a premium price or to pursue low costs. The organization aligns its value chain accordingly, creating manufacturing, marketing, and human resource strategies in the process. On the basis of these strategies, financial targets and budget allocations are set.

The underlying logic here is that a company's strategic options are bounded by the environment. In other words, structure shapes strategy. This "structuralist" approach, which has its roots in the structure-conduct-performance paradigm of industrial organization economics, has dominated the practice of strategy for the past 30 years.[1] According to it, a firm's performance depends on its conduct, which in turn depends on basic structural factors such as number of suppliers and buyers and barriers to entry. It is a deterministic worldview in which causality flows from external conditions down to corporate decisions that seek to exploit those conditions.

Even a cursory study of business history, however, reveals plenty of cases in which firms' strategies shaped industry structure, from Ford's Model T to Nintendo's Wii. For the past 15 years, we have been developing a theory of strategy, known as blue ocean strategy, that reflects the fact that a company's performance is not necessarily determined by an industry's competitive environment.[2] The blue ocean strategy framework can help companies systematically reconstruct their industries and reverse the structure-strategy sequence in their favor.

Blue ocean strategy has its roots in the emerging school of economics called endogenous growth, whose central paradigm posits that the ideas and actions of individual players can shape the economic and industrial landscape.[3] In other words, strategy can shape structure. We call this approach "reconstructionist."

While the structuralist approach is valuable and relevant, the reconstructionist approach is more appropriate in certain economic and industry settings. Indeed, today's economic difficulties have heightened the need for a reconstructionist alternative. The first task of an organization's leadership, therefore, is to choose the appropriate strategic approach in light of the challenges the organization faces. Choosing the right approach, however, is not enough. Executives then need to make sure that their organizations are aligned behind it to produce sustainable performance. Most executives understand the mechanics of making the structuralist approach work, so this article will focus on how to align an organization behind the reconstructionist approach to deliver high and sustainable performance.

What Is the Right Strategic Approach for You?

There are three factors that determine the right approach: the structural conditions in which an organization operates, its resources and capabilities, and its strategic mind-set. When the structural conditions of an industry or environment are attractive and you have the resources and capabilities to carve out a viable competitive position, the structuralist approach is likely to produce good returns (see the exhibit "Choosing the right strategic approach"). Even in a not-so-attractive industry, the structuralist approach can work well if a

Idea in Brief

- There are two types of strategy: structuralist strategies that assume that the operating environment is given and reconstructionist strategies that seek to shape the environment.

- In choosing which of the two is most appropriate for your organization, you need to consider environmental attractiveness, the capabilities and resources you can call on, and whether your organization has a strategic orientation for competing or for innovating. Diversified companies should be comfortable using both approaches.

- Whichever type of strategy is chosen, success will depend on creating an aligned set of strategy propositions targeted at three different sets of stakeholders: buyers, shareholders, and the people working for or with the organization.

- Where the approaches diverge is in the nature of their proper alignment. Structuralist strategies require that all propositions focus on delivering either low cost or differentiation. Reconstructionist strategy propositions aim to deliver both, as exemplified by the cases of the city-state of Dubai, Apple's iTunes, and the charity Comic Relief.

company has the resources and capabilities to beat out the competition. In either case, the focus of strategy is to leverage the organization's core strengths to achieve acceptable risk-adjusted returns in an existing market.

But when conditions are unfavorable and they are going to work against you whatever your resources and capabilities might be, a structuralist approach is not a smart option. This often happens in industries characterized by excess supply, cutthroat competition, and low profit margins. In these situations, an organization should adopt a reconstructionist approach and build a strategy that will reshape industry boundaries.

Even when an industry is attractive, if existing players are well-entrenched and an organization does not have the resources and capabilities to go up against them, the structuralist approach is not going to produce high performance. In this scenario, the organization needs to build a strategy that creates a new market space for itself.

Choosing the right strategic approach

A structuralist approach is a good fit when:	A reconstructionist approach is a good fit when:
• Structural conditions are attractive and the organization has the resources and capabilities to build a distinctive position	• Structural conditions are attractive but players are well-entrenched and the organization lacks the resources or capabilities to outperform them
• Structural conditions are less than attractive but the organization has the resources and capabilities to outperform competitors	• Structural conditions are unattractive and they work against an organization irrespective of its resources and capabilities
• The organization has a bias toward defending current strategic positions and a reluctance to venture into unfamiliar territory	• The organization has an orientation toward innovation and a willingness to pursue new opportunities

When structural conditions and resources and capabilities do not distinctively indicate one approach or the other, the right choice will turn on the organization's strategic mind-set.

When structural conditions and resources and capabilities do not distinctively indicate one approach or the other, the right choice will depend on the organization's strategic mind-set. An organization with an innovative bent and sensitivity to the risks of missing future opportunities will be more successful in adopting a reconstructionist approach. Firms with a bias toward defending current strategic positions and a reluctance to venture outside familiar territory would do better with a structuralist approach.

The Three Strategy Propositions

Whichever approach is chosen, a strategy's success hinges on the development and alignment of three propositions: (1) a value proposition that attracts buyers; (2) a profit proposition that enables the company to make money out of the value proposition; and (3) a people proposition that motivates those working for or with the company to execute the strategy. Where the two approaches diverge is in the alignment of the propositions.

Let's first flesh out our definition of strategy. The value and profit propositions set out the content of a strategy—what a company offers to buyers and how it will benefit from that offering. The people proposition determines the quality of execution. The three strategy propositions correspond to the traditional activity system of an organization: The outputs of an organization's activities are value for the buyer and revenue for itself, and the inputs are the costs to produce them and the people to deliver them. Hence, we define strategy as the development and alignment of the three propositions to either exploit or reconstruct the industrial and economic environment in which an organization operates.

Unless a company creates a complete set of consistent propositions, it is unlikely to produce a high-performing and sustainable strategy. If, for instance, the value and profit propositions are strong, but the people proposition doesn't motivate employees or other constituencies, the organization may experience temporary but unsustainable success. This is the classic case of execution failure. Likewise, an organization that offers a motivating people proposition but lacks a strong value or profit proposition will find itself mired in poor performance. This is formulation failure.

Each proposition may need to address more than one group of stakeholders, as when successful strategy execution rests on the buy-in of not only an organization's employees but also groups outside it, such as supply chain partners. Similarly, a company in a business-to-business industry may have to formulate two value propositions: one for the customer and another for the customer's customers.

Now let's consider where the two approaches diverge. Under the structuralist approach, an organization's entire system of activities, and thus its strategy propositions, needs to be aligned with the distinctive choice of pursuing either differentiation or low cost, each being an alternative strategic position in an industry. A strategy is unlikely to be successful, for instance, if the value and profit propositions are aligned around differentiation but the people proposition is targeted at low cost. Under a reconstructionist strategy approach, high performance is achieved when all three strategy propositions pursue both differentiation and low cost. This alignment in support of differentiation and low cost enables a company to open new market space by breaking the existing value-cost trade-off. It allows strategy to shape structure. It is also alignment that leads to more sustainable strategy, for either approach. While one or two strategy propositions can be imitated, imitating all three, especially the people proposition, is difficult (see the exhibit, "Achieving strategy alignment").

It is the responsibility of an organization's top executives to make sure that each proposition is fully developed and all three are

Achieving strategy alignment

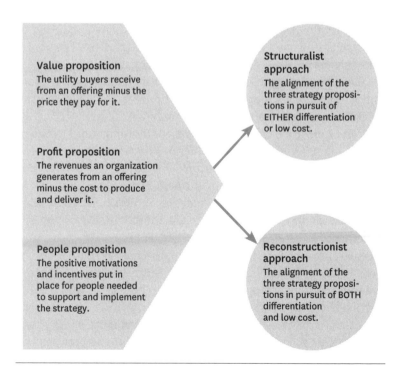

aligned. They alone are suited to this type of broad strategy work; executives with a strong functional bias—marketing, manufacturing, human resources, or other functions—tend to miss the larger strategy picture. The marketing team, for example, may dwell too much on the value proposition and pay insufficient heed to the other two. Similarly, executives with a manufacturing bias may neglect buyer needs or may treat people as a cost variable. If an organization's leadership is not mindful of these tendencies, it is unlikely to develop a full set of properly aligned strategy propositions.

While managers are well-informed about the ways in which structure shapes strategy, there is little knowledge of how to align the three propositions so that strategy can shape structure.[4] In the next section of this article, we look at the city-state of Dubai to show how blue ocean strategy alignment enables an organization to reconstruct the environment. Dubai has redefined the role and activities of its government, yielding one of the fastest-growing economies in the world for two decades.

Achieving Blue Ocean Strategy Alignment

Dubai's success would have been unthinkable 30 years ago. Cement structures were virtually absent in its unforgiving desert. Job opportunities were dismal, and medical services were poor. People lived in huts thatched with palm fronds and tended sheep in relentless heat.

Yet strategic decisions by the emirate's leaders allowed Dubai to overcome seemingly insurmountable structural disadvantages. It has been an island of stability in a politically turbulent region. Only 5% of its revenues now come from oil and natural gas—down from 30% a decade ago. Indeed, Dubai is arguably the only Arab economy that has achieved substantial integration into the global economy outside the hydrocarbon sector and has emerged as a premier tourist and business destination across the globe. Although Dubai, like the rest of the world, is being buffeted by the global financial crisis, and its future depends on how it deals with that crisis, its reconstructionist blue ocean strategic move—aligning the three propositions around differentiation and low cost—has so far brought the emirate unprecedented profitable growth.

Dubai's value proposition has targeted foreign investors whose money fuels the state's economic development. Its profit proposition has allowed the government to benefit and extract revenues from those investors. Dubai's people proposition has motivated its own citizens and its external partners—foreign expatriates—to buy into the country's value and profit propositions and support its strategy.

The value proposition

At the heart of Dubai's success has been a value proposition to foreign investors that is unlike those of other emerging economies. The value proposition begins with a dozen world-class free zones with unbeatable incentives for investors. To achieve differentiation, the government allows 100% foreign ownership and free repatriation of capital and profits. To lower foreign investors' costs, it charges no import or re-export duties. The corporate tax rate for the first 15 to 50 years of operations is zero and can be extended.

To stand out further and simultaneously lower investors' costs, Dubai has also expedited its registration processes, allowing companies to get licensed to conduct business in under a half hour. All documentation is in English, and the emirate's transparent legal system is based on British law (even the chief justice is British). Dubai also offers world-class air, port, and shipping services to make the logistics of doing business more efficient.

Clearly, Dubai has provided a package for foreign investors that is both differentiated and low cost, and it is this combination that has fueled Dubai's strong growth. Compare its value proposition for foreign investors with that of Shanghai, China's biggest commercial center (see the exhibit "Dubai's value proposition"). Shanghai imposes a complex and opaque legal system on foreign investors and requires incoming companies to be familiar with China's norms, customs, and politics. Although Shanghai is one of the largest and fastest-growing economies in the world, Dubai has outperformed it on many measures.

Dubai Strategy Propositions

THE STRATEGY CANVAS IS AN analytical framework we developed in our research on blue ocean strategy, which can be used to express an organization's three strategy propositions. The horizontal axis captures the range of factors organizations offer. The vertical axis depicts the offering level. The strategic profile is a graphic depiction of an organization's relative performance across these key factors. Here we present the strategic profiles for Dubai's three strategy propositions versus those of other emerging markets and Arab economies.

Dubai's value proposition

Shanghai was used as a strategic reference to show how Dubai's value proposition has been compelling to foreign investors despite its much smaller domestic market size.

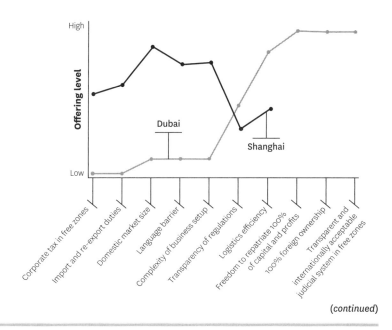

(continued)

Dubai Strategy Propositions

Dubai's profit proposition

Oil-based Arab economies were used as the strategic reference, as these economies are most comparable in terms of their geo-political, social, and government revenue-generating mechanisms.

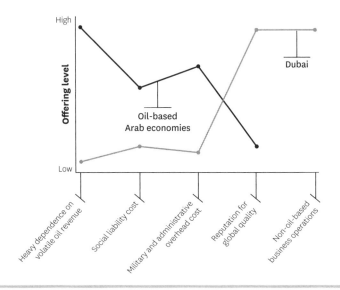

The profit proposition

How does Dubai generate revenues to support the state, given that corporate and personal taxes are negligible? It has done so by finding differentiated ways of generating revenues while also lowering its cost structure. Unlike other Arab governments, Dubai's has been run like a large business enterprise. Its ruler, Sheikh Mohammed bin Rashid al-Maktoum, is frequently quoted as saying, "What's good for business is good for Dubai." Instead of exploiting conventional income channels such as corporate and personal taxes, which would discourage foreign investors, the government has invested in the infrastructure that supports the investors' activities—shipping and port services, transport, tourism, aviation, real estate development, export commerce, and telecommunications. These investments

Dubai's people proposition for citizens

Dubai's past was used as a strategic reference to depict how Dubai's new strategy has made a difference to citizens.

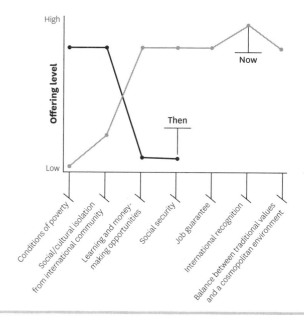

have allowed the government to directly profit from its unique, low-cost value proposition.

One example is DP World, 80% owned by the government through Dubai World. DP World operates the Jebel Ali port and complex in Dubai, where more than 6,000 companies are based. Another is Nakheel, wholly owned by Dubai and now one of the world's biggest real estate developers. Nakheel is slated to develop half of all residential construction projects in the emirate over the next 10 years, allowing the government to profit from the housing needs of foreign employees. And with its ownership of Emirates Airlines, the government makes money on the high volume of business travelers and cargo flowing into Dubai. In serving foreign investors, the government's businesses have acquired the expertise to build global operations that generate yet more money. DP World, for instance, now operates over 50 ports in 31 countries. The result has been strong revenue growth for the state and a global reputation for quality.

Dubai's profit proposition has been not just differentiated: Economic development and government profitability are bolstered by the simultaneous pursuit of low costs. In Dubai, expatriates always remain expatriates: Some 80% of its growing population is now foreign. By restricting citizenship, the government has kept its social liabilities to a minimum. What's more, having made the strategic decision to become a part of United Arab Emirates, Dubai does not need its own military, diplomatic corps, or monetary agency. Abu Dhabi, the UAE capital and possessor of vast oil reserves, bears most of the costs of maintaining the federal government. These factors have combined to form a profit proposition that breaks the existing value-cost trade-off. (See the exhibit "Dubai's profit proposition.")

The people proposition

Dubai has become a cosmopolitan state with more than 1 million people from over 100 countries around the globe. With the onslaught of foreigners, many of them from the West and Asia, how has Dubai preserved its Arab traditions and fostered social tolerance in its citizens? And with no social benefits or citizenship rights to offer, how did Dubai attract the foreign talent central to the government's ability to execute its strategy? By creating people propositions for both constituencies that have delivered differentiated value and lower costs. The people proposition embraces both economic and emotional factors, because these factors can either bring value to people or be a significant cost to their livelihoods.

Let's look first at the people proposition for citizens. They have access to a generous social security system and are virtually guaranteed a government job. They receive extensive state assistance, including medical care, sickness and maternity benefits, child care, free or subsidized education, pensions, unemployment benefits, and in some instances housing and disability benefits, all of which have vastly improved their quality of life.

At the same time, the government has taken measures to preserve Dubai's culture and heritage, in part by promoting virtual boundaries between citizens and foreigners. Citizens receive free plots of land from the government along with interest-free loans or grants to build homes on the outskirts of the city. Their children go to nearby Arabic schools that provide Islamic religious teachings along with modern education. Here, traditional Arab values and cultural norms take center stage. And thanks to a small citizen population and revenues from business investments, the welfare of the people has been funded by the government at no cost to them. (See the exhibit "Dubai's people proposition for citizens.")

Dubai's people proposition for expatriates has been equally compelling. Zero income tax has made their already generous income even more attractive. Housing is also relatively cheap; a recent study revealed that luxury real estate in Dubai costs one-fifth to one-third less than it does in other major commercial centers. Dubai differentiates itself from developing countries like China and India by allowing foreigners to own their properties outright. As these incentives have attracted foreigners, a multicultural environment has sprung up; almost anyone can find a part of their home country experience in Dubai—French wines, Indian saris, Japanese sushi. It even boasts the world's largest indoor ski facility. Dubai's people proposition, in short, has offered foreign talent a rich and unique experience at a low cost.

As Dubai's case illustrates, aligning the three strategy propositions creates reinforcing synergies. With a compelling low-cost and differentiated value proposition, Dubai has attracted foreign businesses, and in serving them has found new and lucrative ways of making money. And because its value and people propositions have attracted foreigners in such numbers, Dubai has been able to create a cosmopolitan environment that is an appealing holiday destination and residence in its own right. Finally, the profit proposition has allowed Dubai to reduce government overhead and use its business revenues to both reinvest in the businesses, thereby giving foreign investors more reason to go there, and provide its own citizens a quality of life their ancestors could not have imagined. Of course, these synergies can be weakened by an external shock like today's global financial crisis. But if and when Dubai succeeds in recovering from the downturn, they will regain strength.

Blue ocean strategy alignment applies not just to governments but to companies and nonprofit organizations as well (see "Comic Relief's Alignment of the Three Strategy Propositions" for more on how it works in the nonprofit sector).

When Strategy Is Not Aligned

Our research suggests that failure to align the three strategy propositions is a key reason why many market-creating innovations fail to become sustainable businesses. Think of the online music provider Napster. Founded in 1999, it had pulled in more than 80 million registered users with its value proposition: simple, easy-to-use software that allowed music files to be indexed, searched, and freely shared across computers throughout the world. Yet within a year, Napster was under siege.

Record labels, worried that the free sharing of music would destroy their sales, approached Napster to work out a revenue-sharing model that would benefit both sides. But excitement over its spectacular growth prevented Napster from appreciating that it needed a people proposition aimed at this critical constituency. Instead of working to build a win-win arrangement with the labels, Napster belligerently declared that it would advance with or without the industry's support. The rest is history: Napster was forced to shut down under a barrage of copyright-infringement suits before it had developed a profit proposition to benefit from its huge user base. Without three aligned strategy propositions, Napster's market-creating innovation failed to deliver commercial success.

Contrast Napster's actions with those of Apple, which launched the iTunes Music Store in 2003 and in the space of five years became the number one music seller in America. Like Napster, iTunes offered a compelling value proposition: Its online music store allowed buyers to freely browse more than 200,000 songs, including exclusive tracks, listen to 30-second samples, and download an individual song

Comic Relief's Alignment of the Three Strategy Propositions

COMIC RELIEF, A UK FUNDRAISING charity, was created in 1985. In 20 years it achieved 96% national brand awareness in an oversaturated industry and has now raised more than £550 million in the UK alone, drawing funds from wealthy donors, low-income families, and even children. It reshaped the world of charity fundraising.

VALUE PROPOSITION. Traditional fundraising charities use feelings of guilt and pity to pull in donations, focus on securing and recognizing large gifts from high-income older donors, and solicit funds year-round. Comic Relief, by contrast, uses a breakthrough approach, Red Nose Day, that combines a day of outrageous community "fun" draising with a star-studded comedy telethon, Red Nose Night. Participants need only buy a red nose for £1 or raise money by doing silly antics that friends sponsor. Even the tiniest donation is valued and recognized. Comic Relief creates this unique experience only every two years to prevent people from feeling bored or hassled. Its value proposition allows donors to make a huge difference while having a great time, at a low cost. Today, Red Nose Day is virtually a national holiday in the UK.

PROFIT PROPOSITION. Comic Relief has an unbeatable profit engine. Red Nose Night, although it's an extravaganza, doesn't cost a penny: The network, the studios, and the stars donate their services. And Red Nose Day likewise has very low costs as the public does the bulk of the fundraising. Unlike traditional UK charities, Comic Relief avoids large advertising costs, thanks to the widespread media attention that Red Nose Day generates. And because Comic Relief makes grants to other charities, rather than introducing competing programs into an already crowded market, its costs are low, creating a differentiated, low-cost profit proposition.

PEOPLE PROPOSITION. With a small number of motivated staff members who are inspired by its value proposition, Comic Relief's people proposition focuses on the public, corporate sponsors, and celebrities whose buy-in is needed to make the value and profit propositions sustainable. The organization gives these constituencies a strong sense of pride and belonging, and a chance to better the world while having fun—at little or no financial cost. Corporate sponsors and celebrities also receive tremendous positive free publicity. The differentiated, low-cost people proposition appeals to those of every socioeconomic stratum.

for 99 cents or an entire album for $9.99. Moreover, iTunes guaranteed high sound quality along with intuitive navigation, search, and browsing functions.

But Apple did not stop there. It built an attractive people proposition for the five major music companies. From the get-go, Apple gained the support of BMG, EMI Group, Sony, Universal Music Group, and Warner Bros. Records by ensuring that music was downloaded with proper copyright protection and paying the music companies 65 cents for every song downloaded. And because iTunes not only earned money for every song downloaded but also drove sales of Apple's already popular iPod, it created a reinforcing cycle of profit across the two platforms. The alignment across iTunes's value, profit, and people propositions not only ushered in a new era of music but is sufficiently hard to imitate that to date no other online music store has been able to establish a firm footing in the industry.

The Napster/iTunes story is all too common. Although innovations aimed at creating new markets clearly have strategic importance for an organization's profitable growth, we all know that many of them result in only temporary success or fail outright. Just ask yourself this question: Which company pioneered or created the video recorder? When we ask MBA and executive audiences this question, the answer is almost always Sony or JVC. When we ask which company first developed the personal computer, the answer is almost always IBM or Apple. These are, of course, the wrong answers. The video recorder was created by a company called Ampex. The PC was created by a company called MITS (Micro Instrumentation and Telemetry Systems). We remember Apple, IBM, Sony, and JVC because they are the ones that first achieved strategy alignment and with it commercial success, establishing their brands in that market space. In 20 years time, what company will we remember as the pioneer of online music, Apple or Napster?

The key lesson here is that managers should not get too excited about innovation per se. It is just the beginning. The real difference between success and failure is strategy alignment. Until executives learn this lesson, billions of dollars will continue to be wasted on market-creating innovations that fail.

The Leadership Challenge

With an increasing number of businesses, governments, and non-profits facing unattractive environmental and structural conditions, leaders can no longer afford to follow the common practice of letting structure drive strategy in all situations. The economic challenges organizations face today only underscore the importance of under-standing how strategy can shape structure. That is not to say, how-ever, that the structuralist approach is no longer relevant. Take any company with multiple businesses. Different business units face dif-ferent structural conditions with different resources and capabilities and have different strategic mind-sets; a structuralist approach will be a better fit for some units, while a reconstructionist approach will be more appropriate for others. The two strategy schools' assump-tions and theories are distinct, and neither is sufficient to deal with the diverse and changing structural and business conditions that organizations face today and in the future. The challenge for lead-ers, therefore, is to ensure that a robust debate takes place on what the right strategic approach for each business should be and then to enter into the spirit of the framework to develop the right strategy for that unit—be it a structuralist competitive strategy model or a reconstructionist blue ocean strategy model.

Are you and your organization ready for that?

Notes

1. See *Industrial Market Structure and Economic Performance*, F. M. Sherer (Chicago: Rand McNally, 1970).

2. See *Blue Ocean Strategy*, W. Chan Kim and Renée Mauborgne (Harvard Business Press, 2005).

3. See, for example, Paul Romer, "The Origins of Endogenous Growth," *Journal of Economic Perspectives*, vol. 8 (Winter 1994).

4. See Michael Porter, "What Is Strategy?" HBR (November–December, 1996); and *Competitive Advantage* (Free Press, 1985).

Originally published in September 2009. Reprint R0909H

Blue Ocean
Leadership

IT'S A SAD TRUTH ABOUT THE WORKPLACE: Just 30% of employees are actively committed to doing a good job. According to Gallup's 2013 *State of the American Workplace* report, 50% of employees merely put their time in, while the remaining 20% act out their discontent in counterproductive ways, negatively influencing their coworkers, missing days on the job, and driving customers away through poor service. Gallup estimates that the 20% group alone costs the U.S. economy around half a trillion dollars each year.

What's the reason for the widespread employee disengagement? According to Gallup, poor leadership is a key cause.

Most executives—not just those in America—recognize that one of their biggest challenges is closing the vast gulf between the potential and the realized talent and energy of the people they lead. As one CEO put it, "We have a large workforce that has an appetite to do a good job up and down the ranks. If we can transform them—tap into them through effective leadership—there will be an awful lot of people out there doing an awful lot of good."

Of course, managers don't intend to be poor leaders. The problem is that they lack a clear understanding of just what changes it would take to bring out the best in everyone and achieve high impact. We believe that leaders can obtain this understanding through an approach we call "blue ocean leadership." It draws on our research on blue ocean strategy, our model for creating new market space by converting noncustomers into customers, and applies its concepts and analytic frameworks to help leaders release the blue ocean of unexploited talent and energy in their organizations—rapidly and at low cost.

The underlying insight is that leadership, in essence, can be thought of as a service that people in an organization "buy" or "don't buy." Every leader in that sense has customers: the bosses to whom the leader must deliver performance, and the followers who need the leader's guidance and support to achieve. When people value your leadership practices, they in effect buy your leadership. They're inspired to excel and act with commitment. But when employees don't buy your leadership, they disengage, becoming noncustomers of your leadership. Once we started thinking about leadership in this way, we began to see that the concepts and frameworks we were developing to create new demand by converting noncustomers into customers could be adapted to help leaders convert disengaged employees into engaged ones.

Over the past 10 years we and Gavin Fraser, a Blue Ocean Strategy Network expert, have interviewed hundreds of people in organizations to understand where leadership was falling short and how it could be transformed while conserving leaders' most precious resource: time. In this article we present the results of our research.

Key Differences from Conventional Leadership Approaches

Blue ocean leadership rapidly brings about a step change in leadership strength. It's distinct from traditional leadership development approaches in several overarching ways. Here are the three most salient:

Focus on acts and activities

Over many years a great deal of research has generated insights into the values, qualities, and behavioral styles that make for good leadership, and these have formed the basis of development programs and executive coaching. The implicit assumption is that changes in values, qualities, and behavioral styles ultimately translate into high performance.

Idea in Brief

The Problem

According to Gallup, only 30% of employees actively apply their talent and energy to move their organizations forward. Fifty percent are just putting their time in, while the remaining 20% act out their discontent in counterproductive ways. Gallup estimates that the 20% group alone costs the U.S. economy around half a trillion dollars each year. A main cause of employee disengagement is poor leadership, Gallup says.

The Solution

A new approach called blue ocean leadership can release the sea of unexploited talent and energy in organizations. It involves a four-step process that allows leaders to gain a clear understanding of just what changes it would take to bring out the best

in their people, while conserving their most precious resource: time. An analytic tool, the Leadership Canvas, shows leaders what activities they need to eliminate, reduce, raise, and create to convert disengaged employees into engaged ones.

Case in Point

A British retail group applied blue ocean leadership to redefine what effectiveness meant for frontline, midlevel, and senior leaders. The impact was significant. On the front line, for example, employee turnover dropped from about 40% to 11% in the first year, reducing recruitment and training costs by 50%. Factoring in reduced absenteeism, the group saved more than $50 million in the first year, while customer satisfaction scores climbed by over 30%.

But when people look back on these programs, many struggle to find evidence of notable change. As one executive put it, "Without years of dedicated efforts, how can you transform a person's character or behavioral traits? And can you really measure and assess whether leaders are embracing and internalizing these personal traits and styles? In theory, yes, but in reality it's hard at best."

Blue ocean leadership, by contrast, focuses on *what acts and activities leaders need to undertake* to boost their teams' motivation and business results, not on *who leaders need to be*. This difference in emphasis is important. It is markedly easier to change people's acts and activities than their values, qualities, and behavioral traits. Of course, altering a leader's activities is not a complete solution, and having the right values, qualities, and behavioral traits matters. But activities are something that any individual can change, given the right feedback and guidance.

Connect closely to market realities

Traditional leadership development programs tend to be quite generic and are often detached from what firms stand for in the eyes of customers and from the market results people are expected to achieve. In contrast, under blue ocean leadership, the people who face market realities are asked for their direct input on how their leaders hold them back and what those leaders could do to help them best serve customers and other key stakeholders. And when people are engaged in defining the leadership practices that will enable them to thrive, and *those practices are connected to the market realities* against which they need to perform, they're highly motivated to create the best possible profile for leaders and to make the new solutions work. Their willing cooperation maximizes the acceptance of new profiles for leadership while minimizing implementation costs.

Distribute leadership across all management levels

Most leadership programs focus on executives and their potential for impact now and in the future. But the key to a successful organization is having empowered leaders at every level, because outstanding organizational performance often comes down to the motivation and actions of middle and frontline leaders, who are in closer contact with the market. As one senior executive put it, "The truth is that we, the top management, are not in the field to fully appreciate the middle and frontline actions. We need effective leaders at every level to maximize corporate performance."

Blue ocean leadership is designed to be applied across the three distinct management levels: *top, middle,* and *frontline.* It calls for profiles for leaders that are tailored to the very different tasks, degrees of power, and environments you find at each level. Extending leadership capabilities deep into the front line unleashes the latent talent and drive of a critical mass of employees, and creating strong distributed leadership significantly enhances performance across the organization.

The Four Steps of Blue Ocean Leadership

Now let's walk through how to put blue ocean leadership into practice. It involves four steps.

1. See your leadership reality

A common mistake organizations make is to discuss changes in leadership before resolving differences of opinion over what leaders are actually doing. Without a common understanding of where leadership stands and is falling short, a forceful case for change cannot be made.

Achieving this understanding is the objective of the first step. It takes the form of what we call as-is Leadership Canvases, analytic visuals that show just how managers at each level invest their time and effort, as perceived by the customers of their leadership. An organization begins the process by creating a canvas for each of its three management levels.

A team of 12 to 15 senior managers is typically selected to carry out this project. The people chosen should cut across functions and be recognized as good leaders in the company so that the team has immediate credibility. The team is then broken into three smaller subteams, each focused on one level and charged with interviewing its relevant leadership customers—both bosses and subordinates—and ensuring that a representative number of each are included.

The aim is to uncover how people experience current leadership and to start a companywide conversation about what leaders do and should do at each level. The customers of leaders are asked which acts and activities—good and bad—their leaders spend most of their time on, and which are key to motivation and performance but are neglected by their leaders. Getting at the specifics is important; the as-is canvases must be grounded in acts and activities that reflect each level's specific market reality and performance goals. This involves a certain amount of probing.

At a company we'll call British Retail Group (BRG), many inter-viewees commented that middle managers spent much of their time playing politics. The subteam focused on that level pushed for clari-fication and discovered that two acts principally accounted for this judgment. One was that the leaders tended to divide responsibility among people, which created uncertainty about accountability— and some internal competitiveness. The result was a lot of finger-pointing and the perception that the leaders were playing people against one another. The subteam also found that the leaders spent much of their time in meetings with senior management. This led subordinates to conclude that their leaders were more interested in maximizing political "face time" and spinning news than in being present to support them.

After four to six weeks of interviews, subteam members come together to create as-is Leadership Profiles by pooling their find-ings and determining, based on frequency of citation, the dominant leadership acts and activities at each level. To help the subteams focus on what really matters, we typically ask for no more than 10 to 15 leadership acts and activities per level. These get registered on the horizontal axis of the as-is canvas, and the extent to which leaders do them is registered on the vertical axis. The cap of 10 to 15 prevents the canvas from becoming a statement of everything and nothing.

The result is almost always eye-opening. It's not uncommon to find that 20% to 40% of the acts and activities of leaders at all three levels provide only questionable value to those above and below them. It's also not uncommon to find that leaders are underinvest-ing in 20% to 40% of the acts and activities that interviewees at their level cite as important.

At BRG, the canvas for senior managers revealed that their cus-tomers thought they spent most of their time on essentially mid-dle-management acts and activities, while the canvas of middle managers indicated that they seemed to be absorbed in protecting bureaucratic procedures. Frontline leaders were seen to be focused on trying to keep their bosses happy by doing things like defer-ring customer queries to them, which satisfied their desire to be in control. When we asked team members to describe each canvas in a tagline, an exercise that's part of the process, they labeled the frontline Leadership Profile "Please the Boss," the middle-manager profile "Control and Play Safe," and the senior manager profile "Focus on the Day-to-Day." (For an example, see the exhibit "What middle managers actually do.")

The implications were depressing. The biggest "aha" for the subteams was that senior managers appeared to have scarcely any time to do the real job of top management—thinking, probing, identifying opportunities on the horizon, and gearing up the organization to capitalize on them. Faced with firsthand, repeated evidence of the shortcomings of leadership practices, the subteams could not defend the current Leadership Profiles. The canvases made a strong case for change at all three levels; it was clear that people throughout the organization wished for it.

2. Develop alternative Leadership Profiles

At this point the subteams are usually eager to explore what effective Leadership Profiles would look like at each level. To achieve this, they go back to their interviewees with two sets of questions.

The first set is aimed at pinpointing the extent to which each act and activity on the canvas is either a cold spot (absorbing leaders' time but adding little or no value) or a hot spot (energizing employees and inspiring them to apply their talents, but currently underinvested in by leaders or not addressed at all).

The second set prompts interviewees to think beyond the bounds of the company and focus on effective leadership acts they've observed outside the organization, in particular those that could have a strong impact if adopted by internal leaders at their level. Here fresh ideas emerge about what leaders could be doing but aren't. This is not, however, about benchmarking against corporate icons; employees' personal experiences are more likely to produce insights. Most of us have come across people in our lives who have had a disproportionately positive influence on us. It might be a sports coach, a schoolteacher, a scoutmaster, a grandparent, or a former boss. Whoever those role models are, it's important to get interviewees to

What middle managers actually do

As- is Leadership Canvases show the activities that employees see leaders engaging in, and the amount of time and energy they think leaders spend on each. The canvas below, for middle managers at the retail company BRG, reveals that people viewed them as rule enforcers who played it safe.

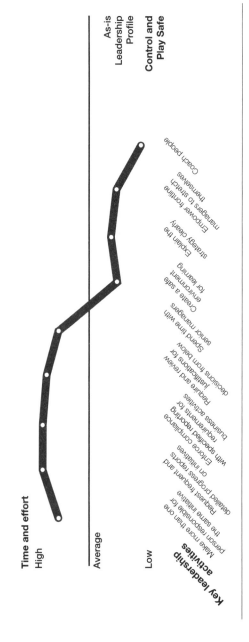

As-is
Leadership
Profile

**Control and
Play Safe**

Coach people

Empower frontline
managers to stretch
themselves

Explain the
strategy clearly

Create a safe
environment
for learning

Spend time with
senior managers

Require and review
justifications for
decisions from below

Enforce compliance
with specified
requirements for
business activities

Request frequent
detailed progress reports
on initiatives

Make more than one
person responsible for
the same initiative

**Key leadership
activities**

Low

Average

**Time and effort
High**

detail which acts and activities they believe would add real value for them if undertaken by their current leaders.

To process the findings from the second round of interviews, the subteams apply an analytic tool we call the Blue Ocean Leadership Grid (see the exhibit by the same name). For each leadership level the interview results get incorporated into this grid. Typically, we start with the cold-spot acts and activities, which go into the Eliminate or Reduce quadrants depending on how negatively interviewees judge them. This energizes the subteams right away, because people immediately perceive the benefits of stopping leaders from doing things that add little or no value. Cutting back on those activities also gives leaders the time and space they need to raise their game. Without that breathing room, a step change in leadership strength would remain largely wishful thinking, given leaders' already full plates. From the cold spots we move to the hot spots,

---

The Blue Ocean Leadership Grid

The Blue Ocean Leadership Grid is an analytic tool that challenges people to think about which acts and activities leaders should do less of because they hold people back, and which leaders should do more of because they inspire people to give their all. Current activities from the leaders' "as-is" profiles (which may add value or not), along with new activities that employees believe would add a lot of value if leaders started doing them, are assigned to the four categories in the grid. Organizations then use the grids to develop new profiles of effective leadership.

Eliminate	Raise
What acts and activities do leaders invest their time and intelligence in that should be eliminated?	What acts and activities do leaders invest their time and intelligence in that should be raised well above their current level?
Reduce	**Create**
What acts and activities do leaders invest their time and intelligence in that should be reduced well below their current level?	What acts and activities should leaders invest their time and intelligence in that they currently don't undertake?

which go into the Raise quadrant if they involve current acts and activities or Create for those not currently performed at all by leaders.

With this input, the subteams draft two to four "to-be" canvases for each leadership level. These analytic visuals illustrate Leadership Profiles that can lift individual and organizational performance, and juxtapose them against the as-is Leadership Profiles. The subteams produce a range of leadership models, rather than stop at one set of possibilities, to thoroughly explore new leadership space.

3. Select to-be Leadership Profiles

After two to three weeks of drawing and redrawing their Leadership Canvases, the subteams present them at what we call a "leadership fair." Fair attendees include board members and top, middle, and frontline managers.

The event starts with members of the original senior team behind the effort describing the process and presenting the three as-is canvases. With those three visuals, the team establishes why change is necessary, confirms that comments from interviewees at all levels were taken into account, and sets the context against which the to-be Leadership Profiles can be understood and appreciated. Although the as-is canvases often present a sobering reality, as they did at BRG, the Leadership Profiles are shown and discussed only at the aggregate level. That makes individual leaders more open to change, because they feel that everyone is in the same boat.

With the stage set, the subteams present the to-be profiles, hanging their canvases on the walls so that the audience can easily see them. Typically, the subteam that focused on frontline leaders will go first. After the presentation, the attendees are each given three Post-it notes and told to put one next to their favorite Leadership Profile. And if they find that canvas especially compelling, they can put up to three Post-its on it.

After all the votes are in, the company's senior executives probe the attendees about why they voted as they did. The same process is then repeated for the two other leadership levels. (We find it easier to deal with each level separately and sequentially, and that doing so increases voters' recall of the discussion.)

After about four hours everyone in attendance has a clear picture of the current Leadership Profile of each level, the completed Blue Ocean Leadership Grids, and a selection of to-be Leadership Profiles that could create a significant change in leadership performance. Armed with this information and the votes and comments of attendees, the top managers convene outside the fair room and decide which to-be Leadership Profile to move forward on at each level. Then they return and explain their decisions to the fair's participants.

At BRG, more than 125 people voted on the profiles, and fair attendees greeted the three that were selected with enthusiasm. The tagline for frontline leaders' to-be profile was "Cut Through the Crap." (Sadly, this was later refined to "Cut Through to Serve Customers.") In this profile, frontline leaders did not defer the vast majority of customer queries to middle management and spent less time jumping through procedural hoops. Their time was directed to training frontline personnel to deliver on company promises on the spot, resolve customer problems, quickly help customers in distress, and make meaningful cross-sales—leadership acts and activities that fired up the frontline workers, were sure to excite customers, and would have a direct impact on the company's bottom line.

"Liberate, Coach, and Empower" was the tagline for middle management's to-be profile. Here leaders' time and attention shifted from controlling to supporting employees. This involved eliminating and reducing a range of oversight activities—such as requiring weekly reports on customer calls received and funds spent on office supplies—that sapped people's energy and kept frontline leaders at their desks. The profile also included new actions aimed at managing, disseminating, and integrating the knowledge of frontline leaders and their staff. In practical terms, this meant spending much more time providing face-to-face coaching and feedback.

The tagline for the to-be profile of senior management was "Delegate and Chart the Company's Future." With the acts and activities of frontline and middle managers reset, senior managers would be freed up to devote a significant portion of their time to thinking

To-be Leadership Canvas

Frontline managers: Serve customers, not the boss

Current activities of BRG's frontline leaders vs. the activities employees think they should be doing

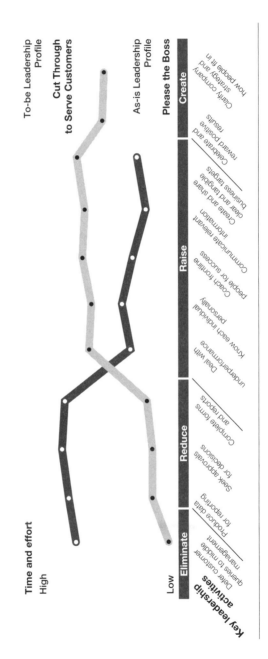

To-be Leadership Canvas

Middle managers: More coaching, less control

Current activities of BRG's midlevel leaders vs. the activities employees think they should be doing

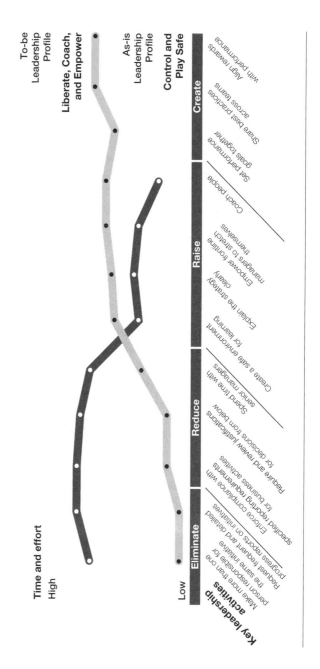

about the big picture—the changes in the industry and their implications for strategy and the organization. They would spend less time putting out fires.

The board members who attended the leadership fair felt strongly that the to-be Leadership Profiles supported the interests of customers as well as shareholders' profit and growth objectives. The frontline leaders were energized and ready to charge ahead. Senior managers went from feeling towed under the waves by all the middle-management duties they had to coordinate and attend to, to feeling as if they could finally get their heads above water and see the beauty of the ocean they had to chart.

The trickiest to-be Leadership Profile was middle management's. Letting go of control and empowering the people below them can be tough for folks in this organizational tier. But the to-be Leadership Profiles of both frontline and senior management helped clear the path to change at this level.

4. Institutionalize new leadership practices

After the fair is over, the original subteam members communicate the results to the people they interviewed who were not at the fair.

Organizations then distribute the agreed-on to-be profiles to the leaders at each level. The subteam members hold meetings with leaders to walk them through their canvases, explaining what should be eliminated, reduced, raised, and created. This step reinforces the buy-in that the initiative has been building by briefing leaders throughout the organization on key findings at each step of the process and tapping many of them for input. And because every leader is in effect the buyer of another level of leadership, all managers will be working to change, knowing that their bosses will be doing the same thing on the basis of input they directly provided.

The leaders are then charged with passing the message along to their direct reports and explaining to them how the new Leadership Profiles will allow them to be more effective. To keep the new profiles top of mind, the to-be canvases are pinned up prominently in the offices of both the leaders and their reports. Leaders are tasked with holding regular monthly meetings at which they gather their

To-be Leadership Canvas

Senior managers: From the day-to-day to the big picture

Current activities of BRG's senior managers vs. the activities employees think they should be doing

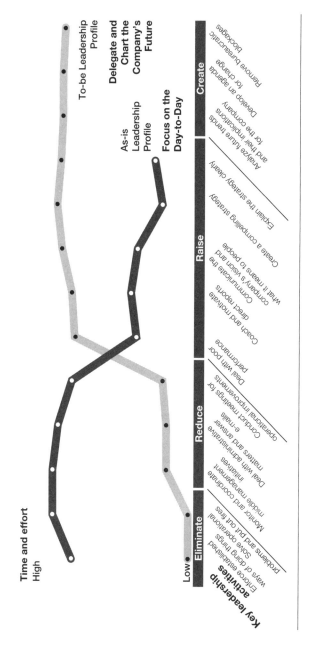

direct reports' feedback on how well they're making the transition to the new profiles. All comments must be illustrated with specific examples. Has the leader cut back on the acts and activities that were to be eliminated and reduced in the new Leadership Profile? If yes, how? If not, in what instances was she still engaging in them? Likewise, is she focusing more on what does add value and doing the new activities in her profile? Though the meetings can be unnerving at first—both for employees who have to critique the boss and for the bosses whose actions are being exposed to scrutiny—it doesn't take long before a team spirit and mutual respect take hold, as all people see how the changes in leadership are positively influencing their performance.

Through the changes highlighted by the to-be profiles, BRG was able to deepen its leadership strength and achieve high impact at lower cost. Consider the results produced just at the frontline level: Turnover of BRG's 10,000-plus frontline employees dropped from about 40% to 11% in the first year, reducing both recruitment and training costs by some 50%. The total savings, including those from decreased absenteeism, amounted to more than $50 million that year. On top of that, BRG's customer satisfaction scores climbed by over 30%, and leaders at all levels reported feeling less stressed, more energized by their ability to act, and more confident that they were making a greater contribution to the company, customers, and their own personal development.

Execution Is Built into the Four Steps

Any change initiative faces skepticism. Think of it as the "bend over—here it comes again" syndrome. While blue ocean leadership also meets such a reaction initially, it counters it by building good execution into the process. The four steps are founded on the principles of fair process: engagement, explanation, and expectation clarity. The power of these principles cannot be overstated, and we have written extensively about their impact on the quality of execution for over 20 years. (See, for example, "Fair Process: Managing in the Knowledge Economy," earlier in this volume.

In the leadership development context, the application of fair process achieves buy-in and ownership of the to-be Leadership Profiles and builds trust, preparing the ground for implementation. The principles are applied in a number of ways, with the most important practices being:

- **Respected senior managers spearhead the process.** Their engagement is not ceremonial; they conduct interviews and draw the canvases. This strongly signals the importance of the initiative, which makes people at all levels feel respected and gives senior managers a visceral sense of what actions are needed to create a step change in leadership performance. Here's a typical employee reaction: "At first, I thought this was just one of those initiatives where management loves to talk about the need for change but then essentially goes back to doing what they've always done. But when I saw that leading senior managers were driving the process and rolling up their sleeves to push the change, I thought to myself, 'Hmm . . . they may just finally mean it.'"

- **People are engaged in defining what leaders should do.** Since the to-be profiles are generated with the employees' own input, people have confidence in the changes made. The process also makes them feel more deeply engaged with their leaders, because they have greater ownership of what their leaders are doing. Here's what people told us: "Senior management said they were going to come and talk to people at all levels to understand what we need our leaders to do and not do, so we could thrive. And I thought, 'I'll believe it when someone comes knocking on my door.' And then they knocked."

- **People at all levels have a say in the final decision.** A slice of the organization across the three management levels gets to vote in selecting the new Leadership Profiles. Though the top managers have the final say on the to-be profiles and may not choose those with the most votes, they are required to provide a clear, sound explanation for their decisions in front of all attendees. Here's some typical feedback: "The doubts we had that our comments were just paid lip service to were dispelled when we saw how our inputs were figured into the to-be profiles. We realized then that our voices were heard."

- **It's easy to assess whether expectations are being met.** Clarity about what needs to change to move from the as-is to the to-be Leadership Profiles makes it simple to monitor progress. The monthly review meetings between leaders and their direct reports help the organization check whether it's making headway. We've found that those meetings keep leaders honest, motivate them to continue with change, and build confidence in both the process and the sincerity of the leaders. By collecting feedback from those meetings, top management can assess how rapidly leaders are making the shift from their as-is to their to-be Leadership Profiles, which becomes a key input in annual performance evaluations. This is what people say: "With the one-page visual of our old and new Leadership Profiles, we can easily track the progress in moving from the old to the new. In it, everyone can see with clarity precisely where we are in closing the gap."

Essentially, the gift that fair process confers is trust and, hence, voluntary cooperation, a quality vital to the leader-follower relationship. Anyone who has ever worked in an organization understands how important trust is. If you trust the process and the people you work for, you're willing to go the extra mile and give your best. If you don't trust them, you'll stick to the letter of the law that binds your contract with the organization and devote your energy to protecting your position and fighting over turf rather than to winning customers and creating value. Not only will your abilities be wasted, but they will often work against your organization's performance.

Becoming a Blue Ocean Leader

We never cease to be amazed by the talent and energy we see in the organizations we study. Sadly, we are equally amazed by how much of it is squandered by poor leadership. Blue ocean leadership can help put an end to that.

The Leadership Canvases give people a concrete, visual framework in which they can surface and discuss the improvements leaders need to make. The fairness of the process makes the implementation and monitoring of those changes far easier than in traditional top-down approaches. Moreover, blue ocean leadership achieves a transformation with less time and effort, because leaders are not trying to alter who they are and break the habits of a lifetime. They are simply changing the tasks they carry out. Better yet, one of the strengths of blue ocean leadership is its scalability. You don't have to wait for your company's top leadership to launch this process. Whatever management level you belong to, you can awaken the sleeping potential of your people by taking them through the four steps.

Are you ready to be a blue ocean leader?

Originally published in May 2014. Reprint R1405C

Red Ocean Traps

The Mental Models That Undermine Market-Creating Strategies

IN AMERICA, CORPORATE PERFORMANCE has been deteriorating for decades. According to Deloitte's landmark study "The Shift Index," the aggregate return on assets of U.S. public companies has fallen below 1%, to about a quarter of its 1965 level. As market power has moved from companies to consumers, and global competition has intensified, managers in almost all industries have come to face steep performance challenges. To turn things around, they need to be more creative in developing and executing their competitive strategies. But long-term success will not be achieved through competitiveness alone. Increasingly, it will depend on the ability to generate new demand and create and capture new markets.

The payoffs of market creation are huge. Just compare the experiences of Apple and Microsoft. Over the past 15 years, Apple has made a series of successful market-creating moves, introducing the iPod, iTunes, the iPhone, the App Store, and the iPad. From the launch of the iPod in 2001 to the end of its 2014 fiscal year, Apple's market cap surged more than 75-fold as its sales and profits exploded. Over the same period, Microsoft's market cap crept up by a mere 3% while its revenue went from nearly five times larger than Apple's to nearly half of Apple's. With close to 80% of profits coming from two old businesses—Windows and Office—and no compelling market-creating move, Microsoft has paid a steep price.

Of course, it's not that companies don't recognize the value of new market spaces. To the contrary, their leaders increasingly are committed to creating them and dedicate significant amounts of money to efforts to do so. But despite this, few companies seem to crack the code. What, exactly, is getting in their way?

In the decade since the publication of the first edition of our book, *Blue Ocean Strategy*, we've had conversations with many managers involved in executing market-creating strategies. As they shared their successes and failures with us, we identified a common factor that seemed to consistently undermine their efforts: their mental models—ingrained assumptions and theories about the way the world works. Though mental models lie below people's cognitive awareness, they're so powerful a determinant of choices and behaviors that many neuroscientists think of them almost as automated algorithms that dictate how people respond to changes and events.

Mental models have their merits. In dangerous times, a robust mental model can help you quickly make decisions that are critical to survival. And we have no issue with the soundness of the mental models that we saw managers apply. They were grounded in knowledge acquired in classrooms and from years of business experience. They help managers respond better to competitive challenges. But our conversations suggest that the mental models managers rely on to negotiate existing market spaces also undermine their ability to create new markets.

In our research and discussions, we've encountered six especially salient assumptions built into managers' mental models. We have come to think of them as red ocean traps, because they effectively anchor managers in red oceans—crowded market spaces where companies engage in bloody competition for market share—and prevent them from entering blue oceans, previously unknown and uncontested market spaces with ample potential. The first two traps stem from assumptions about marketing, in particular an emphasis on customer orientation and niches; the next two from economic lessons on technology innovation and creative destruction; and the final two from principles of competitive strategy that regard differentiation and low cost as mutually exclusive choices. In the following pages, we'll look at each trap in detail and see how it thwarts companies' attempts to create markets.

Idea in Brief

The Problem

To succeed in the long term, companies must find ways to create new markets. Competing in existing markets is growing less profitable. But despite much investment and commitment, companies find it extraordinarily difficult to establish new market spaces.

Why It Happens

Managers' mental models are based on their experiences in existing markets. Though these assumptions and beliefs have worked in the past, they undermine efforts to create new spaces.

The Solution

To avoid being trapped in old markets, managers need to:

- focus on attracting new customers

- worry less about segmentation

- understand that market creation is not synonymous with either technological innovation or creative destruction

- stop focusing on premium versus low-cost strategies

Trap One: Seeing Market-Creating Strategies as Customer-Oriented Approaches

Generating new demand is at the heart of market-creating strategies. It hinges on converting non-customers into customers, as Salesforce.com did with its on-demand CRM software, which opened up a new market space by winning over small and midsize firms that had previously rejected CRM enterprise software.

The trouble is that managers, especially those in marketing, have been quite reasonably brought up to believe that the customer is king. It's all too easy for them to assume, therefore, that market-creating strategies are customer led, which causes them to reflexively stick to their focus on existing customers and how to make them happier.

This approach, however, is unlikely to create new markets. To do that, an organization needs to turn its focus to noncustomers and why they refuse to patronize an industry's offering. Noncustomers, not customers, hold the greatest insight into the points of pain and intimidation that limit the boundary of an industry. A focus on existing customers, by contrast, tends to drive organizations to come up with better solutions for them than what competitors currently offer—but keeps companies moored in red oceans.

Consider Sony's launch of the Portable Reader System (PRS) in 2006. The company's aim was to unlock a new market space in books by opening the e-reader market to a wide customer base. To figure out how to realize that goal, it looked to the experience of existing e-reader customers, who were dissatisfied with the size and poor display quality of current products. Sony's response was a thin, lightweight device with an easy-to-read screen. Despite the media's praise and happier customers, the PRS lost out to Amazon's Kindle because it failed to attract the mass of noncustomers whose main reason for rejecting e-readers was the shortage of worthwhile books, not the size and the display of the devices. Without a rich choice of titles and an easy way to download them, the noncustomers stuck to print books.

Amazon understood this when it launched the Kindle in 2007, offering more than four times the number of e-titles available from the PRS and making them easily downloadable over Wi-Fi. Within six hours of their release, Kindles sold out, as print book customers rapidly became e-reader customers as well. Though Sony has since exited e-readers, the Kindle grew the industry from around a mere 2% of total book buyers in 2008 to 28% in 2014. It now offers more than 2.5 million e-titles.

Trap Two: Treating Market-Creating Strategies as Niche Strategies

The field of marketing has placed great emphasis on using ever finer market segmentation to identify and capture niche markets. Though niche strategies can often be very effective, uncovering a niche in an existing space is not the same thing as identifying a new market space.

Consider Song, an airline launched in 2003 by Delta. Delta's aim was to create a new market space in low-cost carriers by targeting a distinct segment of fliers. It decided to focus on stylish professional women travelers, a segment it figured had needs and preferences different from those of the businessmen and other passengers most airlines targeted. No airline had ever been built around this group. After many focus group discussions with upwardly mobile and professional women, Delta came up with a plan to cater to them with organic food, custom cocktails, a variety of entertainment choices, free in-flight workouts with complementary exercise bands, and crew members dressed in Kate Spade. The strategy was intended to fill a gap in the market. It may well have done that successfully, but the segment proved too small to be sustainable despite competitive pricing. Song flew its last flight in April 2006, just 36 months after its launch.

Successful market-creating strategies don't focus on finer segmentation. More often, they "desegment" markets by identifying key commonalities across buyer groups that could help generate broader demand. Pret A Manger, a British food chain, looked across three different prepared-lunch buyer groups: restaurant-going professionals, fast food customers, and the brown bag set. Although there were plenty of differences across these groups, there were three key commonalities: All of them wanted a lunch that was fresh and healthful, wanted it fast, and wanted it at a reasonable price. That insight helped Pret A Manger see how it could unlock and aggregate untapped demand across those groups to create a commercially compelling new market. Its concept was to offer restaurant-quality sandwiches made fresh every day from high-end ingredients, preparing them at a speed even greater than that of fast food, and delivering that experience in a sleek setting at reasonable prices. Today, nearly 30 years on, Pret A Manger continues to enjoy robust profitable growth in the new market space it established.

Trap Three: Confusing Technology Innovation with Market-Creating Strategies

R&D and technology innovation are widely recognized as key drivers of market development and industry growth. It's understandable, therefore, that managers might assume that they are also key drivers in the discovery of new markets. But the reality is that market creation is not inevitably about technological innovation. Yellow Tail opened a new market (in its case, for a fun and simple wine for everyone) without any bleeding-edge technologies. So did the coffee chain Starbucks and the performing arts company Cirque du Soleil. Even when technology is heavily involved, as it was with market creators Salesforce.com, Intuit's Quicken, or Uber, it is not the reason that new offerings are successful. Such products and services succeed because they are so simple to use, fun, and productive that people fall in love with them. The technology that enables them essentially disappears from buyers' minds.

Consider the Segway Personal Transporter, which was launched in 2001. Was it a technology innovation? Sure. It was the world's first self-balancing human transporter, and it worked well. Lean forward and you go forward; lean back and you go back. This engineering marvel was one of the most-talked-about technology innovations of its time. But most people were unwilling to pay up to $5,000 for a product that posed difficulties in use and convenience: Where could you park it? How would you take it with you in a car? Where could you use it—sidewalks or roads? Could you take it on a bus or a train? Although the Segway was expected to reach breakeven just six months after its launch, sales fell way below initial predictions, and the company was sold in 2009. Not everyone was surprised. At the time of the product's release, a prescient *Time* magazine article about Dean Kamen, Segway's inventor, struck a cautionary note: "One of the hardest truths for any technologist to hear is that success or failure in business is rarely determined by the quality of the technology."

Value innovation, not technology innovation, is what launches commercially compelling new markets. Successful new products or services open market spaces by offering a leap in productivity, simplicity, ease of use, convenience, fun, or environmental friendliness. But when companies mistakenly assume that market creation hinges on breakthrough technologies, their organizations tend to push for products or services that are too "out there," too complicated, or, like the Segway, lacking a necessary ecosystem. In fact, many technology innovations fail to create new markets even if they win the company accolades and their developers scientific prizes.

Trap Four: Equating Creative Destruction with Market Creation

Joseph Schumpeter's theory of creative destruction lies at the heart of innovation economics. Creative destruction occurs when an invention disrupts a market by displacing an earlier technology or existing product or service. Digital photography, for example, wiped out the photographic film industry, becoming the new norm. In Schumpeter's framework, the old is incessantly destroyed and replaced by the new.

But does market creation always involve destruction? The answer is no. It also involves nondestructive creation, wherein new demand is created without displacing existing products or services. Take Viagra, which established a new market in lifestyle drugs. Did Viagra make any earlier technology or existing product or service obsolete? No. It unlocked new demand by offering for the first time a real solution to a major problem experienced by many men in their personal relationships. Grameen Bank's creation of the microfinance industry is another example. Many market-creating moves are nondestructive, because they offer solutions where none previously existed. We've also seen this happen with the social networking and crowd-funding industries. And even when a certain amount of destruction is involved in market creation, nondestructive creation is often a larger element than you might think. Nintendo's Wii game player, for example, complemented more than replaced existing game systems, because it attracted younger children and older adults who hadn't previously played video games.

Conflating market creation with creative destruction not only limits an organization's set of opportunities but also sets off resistance to market-creating strategies. People in established companies typically don't like the notion of creative destruction or disruption because it may threaten their current status and jobs. As a result, managers often undermine their company's market-creating efforts by starving them of resources, allocating undue overhead costs to the initiatives, or not cooperating with the people working on them. It's critical for market creators to head this danger off early by clarifying that their project is at least as much about nondestructive creation as it is about disruption.

Trap Five: Equating Market-Creating Strategies with Differentiation

In a competitive industry companies tend to choose their position on what economists call the "productivity frontier," the range of value-cost trade-offs that are available given the structure and norms of the industry. Differentiation is the strategic position on this frontier in which a company stands out from competitors by providing premium value; the trade-off is usually higher costs to the company and higher prices for customers. We've found that many managers assume that market creation is the same thing.

In reality, a market-creating move breaks the value-cost trade-off. It is about pursuing differentiation and low cost simultaneously. Are Yellow Tail and Salesforce.com differentiated from other players? You bet. But are Yellow Tail and Salesforce.com also low cost? Yes again. A market-creating move is a "both-and," not an "either-or," strategy. It's important to realize this difference, because when companies mistakenly assume that market creation is synonymous with differentiation, they often focus on what to improve or create to stand apart and pay scant heed to what they can eliminate or reduce to simultaneously achieve low cost. As a result, they may inadvertently become premium competitors in an existing industry space rather than discover a new market space of their own.

Take BMW, which set out to establish a new market in urban transport with its launch of the C1 in 2000. Traffic problems in European cities are severe, and people waste many hours commuting by car there, so BMW wanted to develop a vehicle people could use to beat rush-hour congestion. The C1 was a two-wheeled scooter targeting the premium end of the market. Unlike other scooters, it had a roof and a full windshield with wipers. BMW also invested heavily in safety. The C1 held drivers in place with a four-point seat-belt system and protected them with an aluminum roll cage, two shoulder-height roll bars, and a crumple zone around the front wheel.

With all these extra features, the C1 was expensive to build, and its price ranged from $7,000 to $10,000—far more than the $3,000 to $5,000 that typical scooters fetched. Although the C1 succeeded in differentiating itself within the scooter industry, it did not create the new market space in transportation BMW had hoped for. In the summer of 2003, BMW announced it was stopping production because the C1 hadn't met sales expectations.

Trap Six: Equating Market-Creating Strategies with Low-Cost Strategies

This trap, in which managers assume that they can create a new market solely by driving down costs, is the obvious flip side of trap five. When organizations see market-creating strategies as synonymous with low-cost strategies alone, they focus on what to eliminate and reduce in current offerings and largely ignore what they should improve or create to increase the offerings' value.

Ouya is a video-game console maker that fell into this trap. When the company began selling its products, in June 2013, big players like Sony, Microsoft, and Nintendo were offering consoles connected to TV screens and controllers that provided a high-quality gaming experience, for prices ranging from $199 to $419. With no low-cost console available, many people would play video games either on handheld devices or on TV screens connected to mobile devices via inexpensive cables.

An attempt to create a market space between high-end consoles and mobile handhelds, the $99 Ouya was introduced as a low-cost open-source "microconsole" offering reasonable quality on TV screens and most games free to try. Although people admired the inexpensive, simple device, Ouya didn't have the rich catalog of quality games, 3-D intensity, great graphics, and processing speed that traditional gamers prized but the company had to some extent sacrificed to drop cost and price. At the same time, Ouya lacked the distinctive advantage of mobile handheld devices—namely, their play-on-the-go functionality. In the absence of those features, potential gamers had no compelling reason to buy Ouyas.

The company is now shopping itself to acquirers—on the basis of its staff's talent more than the strength of its console business—but as yet hasn't found one.

Our point, again, is that a market-creating strategy takes a "both-and" approach: It pursues both differentiation and low cost. In this framework, new market space is created not by pricing against the competition within an industry but by pricing against substitutes and alternatives that noncustomers are currently using. Accordingly, a new market does not have to be created at the low end of an industry. Instead it can be created at the high end, as Cirque du Soleil did in circus entertainment, Starbucks did in coffee, and Dyson did in vacuum cleaners.

Even when companies create new markets at the low end, the offerings also are clearly differentiated in the eyes of buyers. Consider Southwest Airlines and Swatch. Southwest stands out for its friendly, fast, ground-transportation-in-the-air feel, while stylish, fun designs make Swatches a fashion statement. Both companies' offerings are perceived as both differentiated and low cost.

THE APPROACHES or strategies presented as the red ocean traps are not wrong or bad. They all serve important purposes. A customer focus, for example, can improve products and services, and technology innovation is a key input for market development and economic growth. Likewise, differentiation or low cost is an effective competitive strategy. What these approaches are not, however, is the path to successful market-creating strategies. And when they drive market-creating efforts that involve big investments, they may result in new businesses that don't earn back those investments and that ultimately fail, as we have seen here. That's why it's key to surface and check the mental models and assumptions of the people who are central to executing market-creating strategies. If those models and assumptions are misaligned with the intended strategic purpose of new market creation, you need to challenge, question, and reframe them. Otherwise, you may fall into the red ocean traps.

Originally published in March 2015. Reprint R1503D

About the Authors

W. CHAN KIM and **RENÉE MAUBORGNE** are professors at INSEAD, the world's second-largest business school, and codirectors of the INSEAD Blue Ocean Strategy Institute. They are the authors of *Blue Ocean Strategy*, which is recognized as one of the most iconic and impactful strategy books ever written. The theory of blue ocean strategy has been actively embraced by companies, governments, and nonprofits across the globe and is currently being taught in more than eighteen hundred universities around the world. *Blue Ocean Strategy* is a bestseller across five continents. It has sold over 3.6 million copies and has been published in a record-breaking 44 languages. Kim and Mauborgne are ranked in the top three of the Thinkers50 global list of top management thinkers and were named among the world's top five best business school professors by MBA Rankings. They have received numerous academic and management awards around the globe, including the Nobels Colloquia Prize for Leadership on Business and Economic Thinking, the Carl S. Sloane Award by the Association of Management Consulting Firms, the Leadership Hall of Fame by *Fast Company* magazine, and the Eldridge Haynes Prize by the Academy of International Business, among others. Kim and Mauborgne are Fellows of the World Economic Forum in Davos. Mauborgne is a member of President Barack Obama's Board of Advisors on Historically Black Colleges and Universities (HBCUs). Kim is an advisory member for the European Union and is an advisor for several countries.

Index

EMI, 87
emotional appeal, 62-65
employees
    buy-in and commitment of,
        42-43
    disengagement of, 167-169
    fair process and, 24-29, 34-42
    as hurdle to innovation, 89
    motivation of, 112-113, 121-125,
        153
endogenous growth, 150
engagement, in fair process,
    26, 31
Enron, 67-68
environmental determinism, 144
equity interest model, 89
euro, 67
Executive Jet, 88
expectation clarity, in fair process,
    26, 31
expectations, creating new,
    78-79
explanation, in fair process,
    26, 31

factors of production, 37
fair process, 23-44
    benefits of, 25
    cooperation and, 32, 37, 44
    defined, 25, 29, 30
    innovation and, 40
    in knowledge economy, 37-43
    outcomes and, 23-29
    overcoming mental barriers to,
        43-44
    principles of, 26, 31, 34
    research on, 30
    violations of, 38
Federal Express, 144
focus, of strategy, 95-96
Ford Model T, 136, 140, 146-148

Formule 1, 5, 10-13, 15
functional appeal, 62-65

General Motors (GM), 136, 139
general public, as hurdle to
    innovation, 90-91
Giuliani, Rudolph, 127
global competition, 135, 187
Grameen Bank, 193
growth, sustained, 1

Hayek, Friedrich, 37
Hewlett-Packard (HP), 89
high-growth companies
    driving, 20-22
    research on, 6
    strategic approach of, 1-5, 7
Home Depot, 46-47, 49, 82, 144
Houndsfield, Godfrey, 87

IBM, 14-15, 137, 139, 140
imitation, barriers to, 144-146
imitators, 82
incumbents, 139
industries
    creation of new, 45-69, 131-133
    strategic groups within, 53-55
    structure shaped by strategy,
        149-165
industry assumptions, 5-6
industry conditions, shaping, 4
influencers, 55-58, 123-124
innovation, 45
    adoption hurdles, 73, 89-92
    business model for, 75, 85-89
    challenges of, 71-73
    cost target for, 85-87
    fair process and, 40
    partners for, 87-88

CREATE UNCONTESTED MARKET SPACE AND MAKE THE COMPETITION IRRELEVANT

If you enjoyed reading *The W. Chan Kim and Renée Mauborgne Blue Ocean Strategy Reader*, turn to this expanded edition of the landmark bestseller, *Blue Ocean Strategy*, embraced by business leaders and organizations worldwide.

Now with a new preface and updated chapters and case studies, *Blue Ocean Strategy* argues that lasting success comes not from battling competitors, but from creating "blue oceans"—new, untapped market spaces ripe for growth.

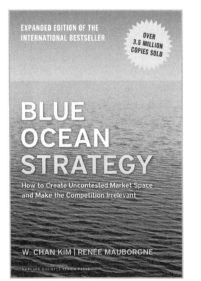

With more than 3.6 million copies sold, and translated into 44 languages, this book charts a bold new path to winning the future.

hbr.org/books

Harvard Business Review Press

Invaluable insights
always at your fingertips

With an All-Access subscription to
Harvard Business Review, you'll get
so much more than a magazine.

Exclusive online content and tools
you can put to use today

My Library, your personal workspace for sharing,
saving, and organizing HBR.org articles and tools

Unlimited access to more than 4,000 articles in the
Harvard Business Review archive

Subscribe today at hbr.org/subnow

The most important management ideas all in one place.

We hope you enjoyed this book from *Harvard Business Review*. For the best ideas HBR has to offer turn to HBR's 10 Must Reads Boxed Set. From books on leadership and strategy to managing yourself and others, this 6-book collection delivers articles on the most essential business topics to help you succeed.

HBR's 10 Must Reads Series

The definitive collection of ideas and best practices on our most sought-after topics from the best minds in business.

- Change Management
- Collaboration
- Communication
- Emotional Intelligence
- Innovation
- Leadership
- Making Smart Decisions

- Managing Across Cultures
- Managing People
- Managing Yourself
- Strategic Marketing
- Strategy
- Teams
- The Essentials

hbr.org/mustreads